STARTING OUT WITH
Microsoft Visual C++

Doug White

University of Northern Colorado

Scott/Jones, Inc.
P.O. Box 696
El Granada, California 94018
Voice: 650-726-2436
Facsimile: 650-726-4693
E-mail: marketing @ scottjonespub.com
Web page: //www.scottjonespub.com

ISBN: 1-57676-069-3

Starting Out With Microsoft C++ by Doug White

Copyright © 2001 by Scott/Jones, Inc

All rights reserved. No part of this book may be reproduced or transmitted in any form without written permission of the publisher.

ISBN: 1-57676-069-3

1 2 3   Z Y X

The publisher wishes to acknowledge the memory and influence of James F. Leisy. Thanks, Jim. We miss you.

Text Design: Cecelia G. Morales
Cover Design: Stephen Adams
Copyediting: Janice Raje
Book Manufacturing: Von Hoffmann Graphics

Scott/Jones Publishing Company

Publisher: Richard Jones
Production Management: Heather Bennett
Editorial Group: Richard Jones, Denise Simon, Mike Needham, Michelle Windell, and Patricia Miyaki
Marketing & Sales: Victoria Judy, Hazel Dunlap, Donna Cross, Page Mead, and Michelle Windell
Business Operations: Michelle Robelet, Cathy Glenn, and Natascha Hoffmeyer

A Word About Trademarks

Additional Titles of Interest from Scott/Jones

Standard Version of Starting Out with C++, Third Edition
Brief Version of Starting Out with C++, Third Edition
Alternate Version of Starting Out with C++, Second Edition
        by Tony Gaddis

Lab Manual to Accompany the Standard Version of Starting Out with C++, Third Edition
        by Dean Defino and Michael Bardzell

Lab Manual to Accompany the Alternate Version of Starting Out with C++, Second Edition
        by Judy Walters, Dean Defino, and Michael Bardzell

C by Discovery, Third Edition
        by L.S. and Dusty Foster

Assembly Language for the IBM PC Family, Third Edition
        by William B. Jones

Advanced Visual Basic, Second Edition
        by Kip Irvine

Introduction to Programming with Visual Basic 6, Second Edition
        by Gary Bronson

The Visual Basic 6 Coursebook, Fourth Edition
QuickStart to JavaScript
ShortCourse in HTML
QuickStart to DOS for Windows 9X
        by Forest Lin

The Complete Computer Repair Textbook, Third Edition
        by Cheryl Schmidt

The Windows 2000 Server Lab Manual
        by Gerard Morris

Windows 2000 Professional Step-by-Step
Essential Windows 2000 Professional Step-by-Step
        by Debbie Tice and Leslie Hardin

The Windows 2000 Professional Textbook
A Short Prelude to Programming
A Prelude to Programming
        by Stewart Venit

Access 2000 Guidebook, Third Edition
        by Maggie Trigg and Phyllis Dobson

HTML for Web Developers
Server-Side Programming for Web Developers
        by John Avila

Developing Web Applications with Active Server Pages
        by Thom Luce

Computing with Java, Second Edition
Computing with Java, Alternate Second Edition
Internet Applications with the Java 2 Platform
From Objects to Components with the Java Platform
        by Art Gittleman

Acknowledgements

The author would like to thank the individuals who reviewed this manuscript and made it better, Vicki Phillips, my students in BACS 286, Heather Bennett, and Janice Raje. I would also like to thank Hazel Dunlap and Richard Jones, who made this book possible.

This book is dedicated to Gene and Lottie White, who gave all they could without ever a thought for themselves.

Contents

1 Introduction to Compilers

The world of technology is an exciting and dynamic place. All of the players must constantly work to maintain and upgrade their skills if they wish to remain viable in this field. This book is directed toward you, students of programming who wish to get a quick overview of how to use a specific tool to accomplish your programming goals. In this case, the tool is Microsoft's Visual C++ Standard Edition, which is bundled with this text.

This book will assist you with using the technology, but it is not designed to teach you how to program in Visual C++. It covers a variety of topics including the following:

- Installing Visual C++ Standard Edition 6.0
- Creating C++ files
- Compiling
- Debugging source code for both syntax and logic errors
- Creating different file types in Visual C++ Standard Edition 6.0
- Working with projects and workspaces
- Starting to use Visual C++ Standard Edition 6.0 quickly through tutorials

Overview of Compilers

In programming, a compiler is a tool, an engine that works on your behalf to process instructions and allow you to deal with the various components that make up a computer. The compiler's job is to make sure you follow the basic rules of the language, and if you make up new rules, to provide enough information that the compiler can translate your instructions into language the components can understand.

Thus, a compiler traces the following set of steps:

List 1.1

1. Get the set of instructions from you.

2. Review the instructions to see if any violate the rules.

3. If all the rules are obeyed, create a working file in the language of the computer (machine language).

4. Attach to the working file full instructions for any shortcuts you may have used.

5. Assemble a final file in machine language.

Example 1.1

Suppose you have a robot that can manufacture just about anything you ask for if you write a set of instructions. So, you decide to try and have the robot manufacture a cheeseburger. Many of the components can simply be described by name and the robot will know what you want. So, you write some instructions:

Take a bun and split it in half.
Take one quarter pound ground beef patty.
Take a slice of cheddar cheese.
Cook ground beef patty until internal temperature is 130 degrees.
Place ground beef patty on bottom of bun.
Place cheese on ground beef patty.
Place top of bun on cheese.

Now, most any human could follow a set of instructions like this, but the robot needs specific instructions. Since you don't want to reinstruct the robot every time on some common actions such as "cook" or "take," these actions might be included in a library of common actions that come with the robot when you buy it from Acme Robots, Inc. on the web. The compiler does this task in the sense that a great many common actions (often referred to as ANSI standards) are included with the C++ compiler you are using. These instructions are included with Visual C++ and are called a library file. Thus, the compiler will take your instructions, find any terms you have used that aren't defined (maybe secret sauce in the example), and then ask you to define them, do away with them, or change them so that they work with the compiler. Any terms that the compiler understands can then be associated with the complex instructions needed to accomplish the task. This type of operation will save you, the programmer, a lot of time since you can simply say "cook" instead of giving a full explanation of how to cook each given thing as it comes up.

Compiler Files

Every compiler uses a set of files to perform its operations. There are four main files that exist on almost every compiler for almost every programming language:

- The source code
- The linked/library file
- The object file
- The executable file

The Source Code

Source code is the heart of any program. It is the set of instructions that you will develop on your own for processing by the compiler. Source codes on Intel-based platforms are often developed in ASCII.

Definition 1.1

ASCII refers to the American Standard Code for Information Interchange, a system of encoding letters, numbers, and symbols (e.g. ∞) into a set of 8-bit binary numbers. This system is used by all the Intel-based PCs and is common throughout the world. Many foreign character sets have also been added into the ASCII set. The most common terminology for this is DOS TEXT or TEXT files.

Figure 1.1

C++ Source
Code File Icon

ASCII files can be created with just about any word processor or even with simple text editors such as Notepad. Many modern compilers attempt to go beyond this approach and incorporate their own environments for developing source code.

In Visual C++, the source code files have an extension to make them easy for you (and the system) to identify. The extension is **.cpp**. This extension on a filename (for example, **myProg.cpp**) tells the programmer that this is a C++ source code file, and it tells the Microsoft Windows-based operating systems to use the Visual C++ editor to manipulate the file. These files usually associate with an icon that looks like Figure 1.1.

You should always adhere to the standards for files of a given type as this will help you locate the files later and make sure that your compiler is able to interpret them correctly. Visual C++ may mishandle C++ programs that do not have the **.cpp** extension. If you use Visual C++ to create source code files, they will have this extension by default.

The Object File

Object files are created by the compiler and often have the extension **.obj**. These are files that have been processed through the first series of steps by the compiler (steps 1 and 2 in List 1.1). This file simply contains the source code that you have created, but now the source code has been converted into machine language and the file itself is no longer readable by you. **NOTE:** If Step 2 is not completed successfully (that is if you have broken some of the rules of the compiler), the object file will not be created and you cannot proceed until you have overcome the problems. This process is called **debugging**.

Definition 1.2

Debugging is the process of removing errors from the source code. Debugging comes in two forms: syntax debugging and logic debugging. Syntax debugging is working to get your source code into a form the compiler will accept. Logic debugging is testing to determine if errors in programming are creating errors in output, even though the program instructions adhere to the rules of syntax.

The Library File

When an object file is created, the compiler must also create a **library file** of instructions. These are the detailed instructions described in example 1.1 such as "cook" and "take." This library file (and there may be multiple library files opened) will contain all the additional source code necessary for the compiler to process your instructions. Thus, when you issue a simple command like "cook" you hope that someone else has written the detailed instructions explaining how to "cook" and that there is a library containing these instructions. In most programming languages, these types of commands are called **keywords**.

Definition 1.3

Keywords are reserved words that refer to predefined actions in a programming language.

The Executable File

When the entire compilation process is complete, the object file and the needed pieces from the library file are merged together to create a machine-language **executable file**. For most compilers, this executable file contains all the needed instructions to actually "run" the program. This type of file most often has the extension **.exe** in Intel-based systems and is a common sight on any computer. A true executable file is not readable by most individuals. The **.exe** file itself is stored in binary form and copies of the file may be distributed to anyone who needs to run it. The compiler itself is an example of an executable file as you are running a program when you use the compiler system. The most common end-user terminology for an executable file is an **application**.

Various C++ Compilers Currently Available

There are a great many C++ compilers available on the market today. As this is the most common application development language, many companies want to provide products to meet the needs of programmers. The trend is toward development kits or programming workbenches in which many useful tools are gathered to facilitate the rapid and easy development of programs. Available products range from freeware compilers that provide only a means to create executables to expensive work environments designed for commercial application development. The following list of some of the compilers and the operating systems for which they were designed is not exhaustive but constitutes an overview of the tools available today.

Compiler (alphabetical except freeware)	Operating Systems Supported
Borland C++ Development Tools	Windows
Borland Turbo C++ Visual Edition	Windows
CodeWarrior	MAC, UNIX, BeOs

DeltaPro C++	UNIX
IBM Visual Age C++	Windows, AIX, Solaris
Intel C/C++	Windows
Microsoft Visual C++	Windows
NDP C/C++	OS/2
Symantec C++	Windows
Watcom C/C++	Windows, DOS, OS/2
Zortech C++	(MAC, DOS)
GNU Freeware	UNIX
DJGPP Freeware	UNIX

In addition, there are numerous compilers available for C++, which support mainframe operating systems such as MVS and mini-computer operating systems such as OS/400. There are most certainly additional C++ compilers available, but those listed are common.

Microsoft Versions of Visual C++

As with any software, Microsoft supports and modifies its C++ compiler on a regular basis. In addition, Microsoft uses a segmentation strategy to appeal to different market segments.

The version bundled with this book was known as the **Learning Edition** in Version 5.0. Its name has been changed to the **Standard Edition** in Version 6.0. This section provides a general description of the various versions currently available.

The current version of Microsoft Visual C++ is version 6.0. Three previous versions and their various incarnations are still supported by Microsoft:
- Version 5.0
- Version 4.2
- Version 4.0

This version of the programming environment is included in both Visual C++ 6.0 and Visual Studio 6.0. There is no difference in the two except that the Visual Studio version also includes Visual Basic (a programming language) and Visual Interdev (a web development language).

Microsoft Visual C++ is a development environment rather than simply a compiler. This environment includes an editor and many basic tools as well as **Microsoft Foundation Classes** to support the development of both traditional batch-oriented applications and **WIN32 Applications**.

Definition 1.4

Microsoft Foundation Classes provide prewritten tools in C++ to allow developers to quickly build new applications by utilizing program source code developed by others.

Definition 1.5

WIN32 Applications are programs that run in the Windows 95; Windows 98; Windows 2000; and Windows NT environments. These are applications, such as MS-Word, or other programs designed to run using Windows as a platform.

Three current editions of Visual C++ 6.0 are available from Microsoft at this time.

- Enterprise Edition
- Professional Edition
- Standard Edition

All three versions include the C++ compiler and basic tools, but the editions are designed for different types of users.

Standard and Introductory Edition

This edition supports users and students in the development of small-scale applications and is bundled with this book. While this version does not contain all the tools for net development, it is sufficient for most courses in C++ and for beginning/intermediate users of the language. Most C++ courses focus on the development of programming skills rather than on the development of complex real-world applications. The standard edition includes tutorials on code development to assist new users and is designed with reduced cost in mind rather than speed, which becomes more important in commercial applications.

Professional Edition

This version is targeted at commercial application developers and high-end students of C++ who are developing complex Windows applications. It has all the features of the Standard Edition except the tutorials, and also supports many database applications, Windows 2000, faster compile times, and other speed increases.

Enterprise Edition

This version is targeted at commercial application developers who are also using C++ to develop e-commerce solutions. In addition to all the features of the Professional Edition, it adds Microsoft SQL Server (a database product); various database tools, and secure server development tools. This product supports almost any sort of C++ development application and is the newest in the Visual C++ line.

Installing the Visual C++ Introductory Edition 6.0 Software on your Computer

Microsoft has created an edition of Visual C++ 6.0 for inclusion with textbooks. This section walks you through installing the software on an personal computer running Windows 95 or Windows 98. If your course involves the use of other platforms (such as Linux, NT, or Macintosh) you may need to consult your instructor for special instructions on how to use the compiler. You may also have access to this or other Visual C++ products on your local area network. It is most likely your computer lab or work environment will not allow you to install this product on a public workstation. If you are working in an environment of this type, you should consult your network administrator or instructor regarding where and how you may use this product.

You should have received a CD-ROM disk with the book you purchased. This CD contains the files for the Standard Edition of Visual C++. Before you install any new software on your system, you should back up all the important files on your hard disk in order to protect them from any problems that might occur during the install.

First, you should close all programs that are running. Other programs may interfere with the installation or may have their operation corrupted by the install process. All screen shots are from Windows 98.

1. Insert the CD in the CD drive on your machine and close the drive. This should cause the Windows XX feature to take over and start the setup program (it may take a few minutes for autorun to appear to do anything).

    If the setup screen appears, skip to Step 3. If the setup screen does not appear, you may not have autorun enabled. You will need to run the program manually as described in Step 2.

2. If autorun has failed, click the **Start** button, choose **Run**, and type **x:\setup** in the field shown in the resulting dialog box (where **x** is the letter of your CD-ROM drive. To find the letter of your CD-ROM drive, look in the **Windows Explorer** directory as shown in Figure 1.3 on page 8). The most common letter for a CD-ROM drive is D, but it can be any letter from A to Z.

Figure 1.2

The Run Item

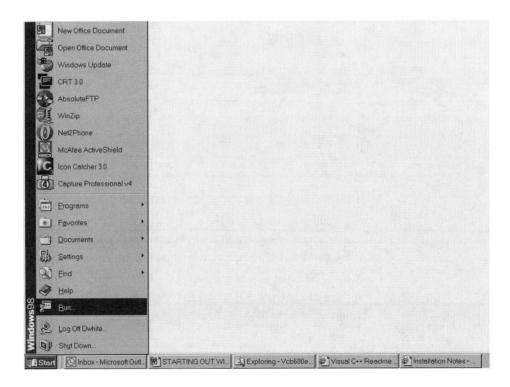

Figure 1.3

Finding the CD-ROM Drive on Explorer

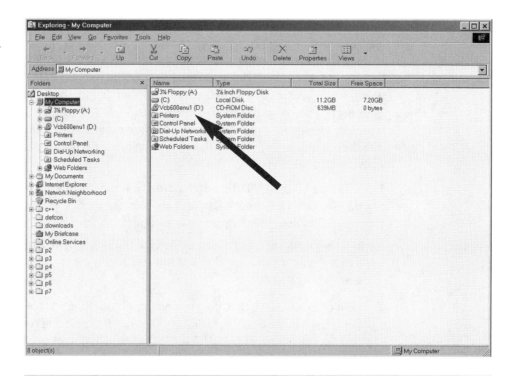

Figure 1.4

The Manual Setup

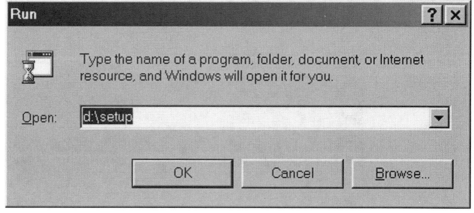

3. You should see the main setup screen as shown in Figure 1.5.

    You may want to view the readme file, which contains notes and other information that may be important to your installation of this product. If you do, click the **View Readme** button and read the file. Otherwise, click **Next**.

4. You will be asked to read and accept the license for the product. Read the license and if you agree, then click the **I accept** button as shown in Figure 1.6. A **Next** button will reappear and you can click **Next**.

Figure 1.5

The Main Setup
Screen

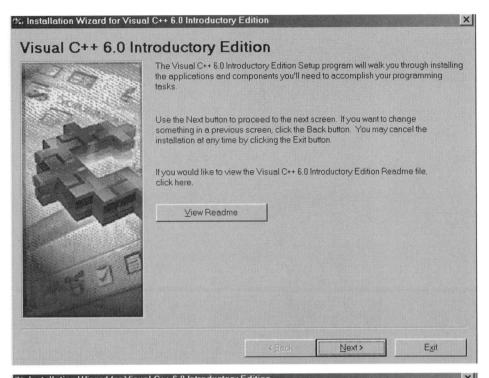

Figure 1.6

The License
Agreement

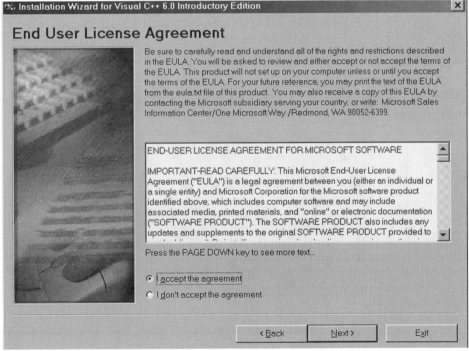

Figure 1.7

The User ID

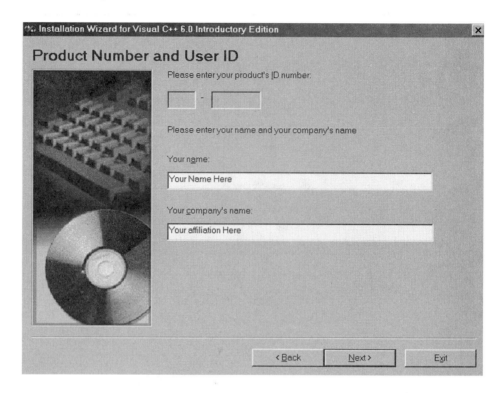

5. You will be asked to enter your name and your company name, which will be integrated with the files for Visual C++. (See Figure 1.7 on page 10.) The product ID is not needed for this Introductory Edition so you needn't worry about it.

Figure 1.8

The Continue
Button

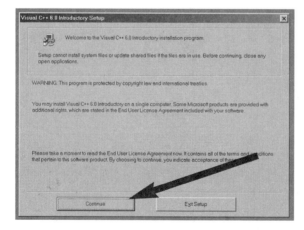

6. You should see the setup screen starting and a warning about closing all other programs. Closing all other applications is a good idea before continuing. When you are ready, press the **Continue** button as shown in Figure 1.8.

Figure 1.9

The Product ID Screen

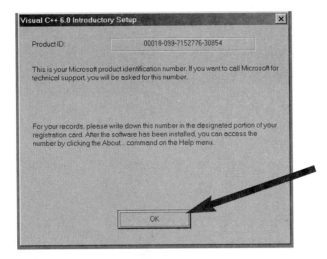

Figure 1.10

The Options Screen

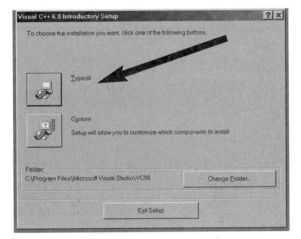

7. You will then see the Product ID screen (Figure 1.9). The number shown is a reference for Microsoft. Click **OK**.

8. You will then come to an install screen that asks for **Typical** or **Custom** and allows you to choose where to install the files. (See Figure 1.10.) Set the location if you want something different by choosing the **Change Folder** button. If you are an experienced user, you can choose custom install, but most students should choose **Typical** and allow the install in the default directory. **NOTE:** The drive letters on your machine may be different than the example.

9. The program will then check for disk space and start to copy files. This may take a while but you can watch the progress. (See Figure 1.11 on page 12.)

10. Barring some complication, you may receive some informational messages. Read the messages and click **OK** to proceed.

Figure 1.11

The Install
Progress Screen

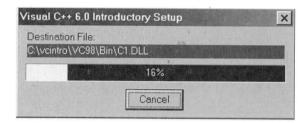

Figure 1.12

The Successful
Install Screen

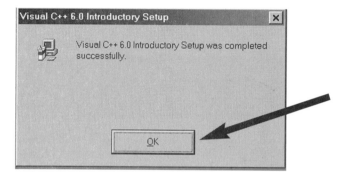

Figure 1.13

The
Documentation
Install Screen

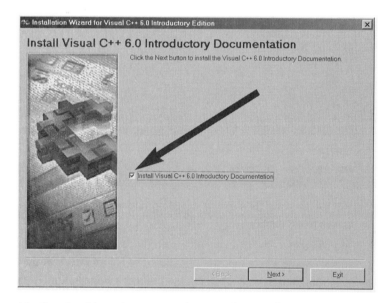

11. You should receive a notice that says the installation was completed successfully. Click **OK** to acknowledge this. (See Figure 1.12 on page 12.)

12. A screen allowing you to read introductory documentation will then appear (Figure 1.13). This screen has a small check box offering to install this documentation.

    If you have disk space, I recommend allowing the documentation to install as this may help you if you have difficulty with the software later.

Figure 1.14

The Close
Applications
Screen again

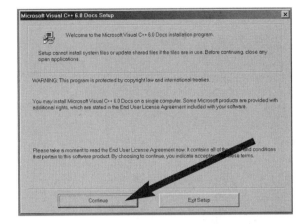

Figure 1.15

The Product ID
Screen again

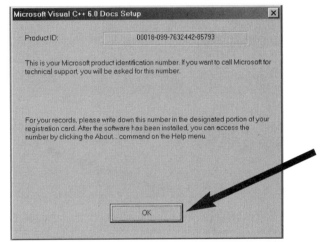

If you don't want the documentation, click the **Install** box to remove the check. Then click **Next**.

13. You will then get another warning about closing all the other running applications (see Figure 1.14). Most likely you haven't opened an application since you started all this, but if you did, close it and then click **Continue**.

14. You will then see the Product ID screen again (Figure 1.15 on page 14). Since you already wrote it down, click **OK**.

15. Another end user license agreement will appear (screen not shown)and after you have read it and agree, click **I Agree**.

16. Another setup box (Figure 1.16 on page 14) will appear and you are again offered the chance to change the location. The only option here is **Typical** and again, most students should use the defaults.

Figure 1.16

The Setup
Screen

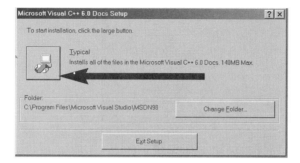

Figure 1.17

The Doc Install
Progress

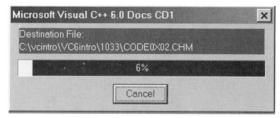

Figure 1.18

The Successful
Installation
Screen

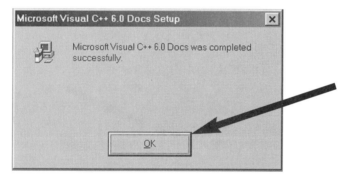

Figure 1.19

The
Congratulations
Screen

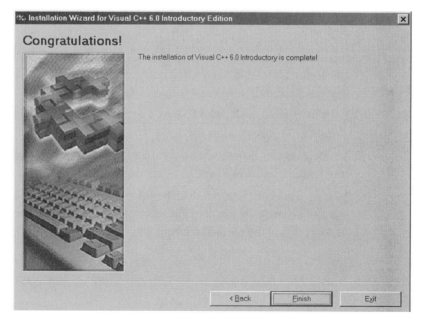

17. Setup will check the disk space and then begin installing files. This may take some time. (See Figure 1.17.)

18. You will finally receive the "successful installation" screen (Figure 1.18). Click **OK**.

19. You should then see the Congratulations! screen (Figure 1.19). Click **Finish**.

This completes the installation. The most common problems students encounter are disk space and previous installation problems. If you are short of disk space, omit the documentation sections as a first option. If you still don't have enough space, you will be forced either to delete files from the hard drive, buy more disk space, or elect not to install the program. If you have some other version of Visual C++ or Visual Studio, you should check with your instructor as to how this many affect you in the course you are taking. The three commercial versions of Visual C++ 6.0 are more complete than the introductory version and are generally preferable, but check with your instructor to make sure.

Support for Visual C++ on the Web

As with most texts today, we provide additional information and source code downloads for all the tutorials in this text. In addition, addenda or other errata for this book may be found on the web. We will also provide a listing of common sources of help for Visual C++ and Visual Studio users on the Internet.

Support for this text

doug.white@acm.org	The author's email address
cislab.unco.edu/dwhite	The author's website

Support for Visual C++

msdn.Microsoft.com/visualc/	Microsoft's Visual C++ site
www.functionx.com/visualc/	A site supporting complex application development
www.tek-tips.com	A site with many forums including MSVC++
codeguru.earthweb.com	A C++ programming site

2 Creating Source Code Files

Programmers spend most of their time working with source code files. It's a good idea to find a text editor that's both functional and comfortable for you. For this reason, many programmers use the same editor (e.g. TECO, VI, or SOS) for many years on different mainframes and with various programming languages. Today, your first inclination may be to use a familiar word processing program to generate source code. This is not a good idea. Most compiler systems today function within an environment designed for development in a specific language. Visual C++ includes a development environment (editor) for the development of source codes in Visual C++.

There are any number of ways you can generate source code files, and any text editor (including TECO, VI, and SOS) will allow you to create C++ source code, but only an environment can provide all the tools to make this process efficient and easy, particularly for beginning programmers. This chapter provides you information on the following topics:

- ASCII source files
- Developing source files using Visual C++ 6.0 Standard Edition
- Managing source files
- Developing a source file in a practice exercise

ASCII Source Files

As mentioned earlier, ASCII is a basic symbol set used for Intel-based systems. C++, like most other programming languages of the past (ASCII is a recent development), processes text files that can be generated using any application capable of creating them. One advantage of ASCII text files is that files can be exchanged and read by almost any ASCII-based product.

There are no advanced formatting tools for dealing with ASCII files. This means you don't have to worry about underlines, fonts, or other formatting features. In fact, it's not possible to include formatting in an ASCII text file since only ASCII symbols are supported.

WINXX* supports filenames that are similar to LINUX/UNIX type** filenames. Very limited rules govern their use. Most file extensions are three spaces long, based on the MS-DOS requirement of a filename with no more than eight characters on the left of the "dot" (.) and three on the right. Common extensions are: .exe, .txt, .doc, .cpp, and so forth.

Today, WINXX-based systems recognize files based on "associations" that use the MS-DOS type extensions to recognize file types. Thus, if you decide to use some unconventional system for your files on a WINXX system, you may find the system won't recognize them automatically. This may cause a great deal of difficulty for other users, and it may actually make locating your own files difficult later if you forget what sort of file naming system you invented.

If you do decide to edit your C++ source files with something other than the Visual C++ environment editor, you should take care to save your files as ASCII, DOS Text, MS-DOS Text, Plain Text, or Text type files with the extension **.cpp**. Most editing software will attempt to put other extensions on the files such as **.txt** or **.asc**, when you save them so you must specify **.cpp** as the type. Most C++ compilers will recognize any filename, but varying filenames and extensions create complications for beginning programmers.

The name on the left side of the decimal place is more open to discussion. Many programmers come up with complex schema for naming files and/or follow what they were taught or what is required by their company. Some production environments (such as commercial programming operations) may impose a given schema for consistency among all programmers. They may use a different schema for test applications than for finalized production applications.

One convention that has become a standard in WINXX systems is the convention that all applications have a SETUP.EXE file in them. This way, general public users always know how to start installing an application without instructions.

The author suggests a standard approach for students: saving source files using a significant portion of your last name and the assignment number. Thus, the author's files for programming assignments two and five (respectively) look like this:

whitePII.cpp and **whitePV.cpp**

Some people have lengthy last names that, while they are supported, create unwieldy filenames. For those situations, use eight letters and the program name. It's good to have a system that works for you. Some other schema may be more appropriate for you and the environment in which you work, so please consult with your instructor.

∗ Programmers and other information professionals may refer to WINXX to imply any version of the Windows operating system.

∗∗ Linux, by Linus Torvalds, and Unix (the basis for Linux) are popular among network administrators and programmers. Linux currently provides the main competition for Windows.

Mainframe and minicomputers do not follow these rules. Keep in mind that this text focuses on the use of Intel-based systems running WINXX. So, later, don't be surprised by filenames that defy all recognition if you are using VMS, MVS, OS/400 or other operating systems. Also, don't forget that the conventions used here are not rules, merely guidelines to help you get started programming.

Common C++ Usages and Conventions

In C++, as in any language, there are rules, standards, and conventions that programmers need to understand if they are to use the language successfully. While it is not the purpose of this text to instruct you in the use of C++, some common features should be discussed with regard to development of source codes in C++.

Case Sensitivity in C++

C++ is a case-sensitive programming language. For many programmers, this is a difficult issue. Often in the past, programmers used all uppercase or all lowercase letters for everything and never even thought about case. In C++, names and other usages are all subject to case. This means that a ≠ A and doug ≠ Doug in the eyes of C++ and the C++ compiler. Beginning programmers need to exhibit extra care in dealing with this issue, as many syntax errors will result purely due to the misuse of case in source code.

In ASCII, every symbol has a number that is unique to that symbol. A small 'a' has the ASCII number (converted to decimal for convenience) 97 and a capital A has the ASCII number 65. Since the computer uses binary numbers for everything, it cannot even consider that a = A since 97 ≠ 65 under any circumstances. It is critical that you adopt a convention for naming things in C++ that will allow you to remember how you deal with this issue. We will discuss some rules and some conventions that are used in C++ to help you get started.

Keywords

Every programming language has specific instructions called keywords that are standard in the language. If you recall Example 1.1, you will remember that our robot knew how to "cook" and how to "take" things. In the same manner, C++ has many keywords that are defined for the compiler.

InfoBox

Programmers are often paranoid about using keywords by accident. Beginning programmers usually worry that they have accidentally used a keyword to name something (thus creating a horrible syntax error). One thing to note about C++ is that the ANSI standard version of C++ contains no keywords that are uppercase or even partially uppercase (e.g. while is a keyword; While is not a keyword).

It is worth noting that when programmers define new keywords they can break all the rules and create keywords that don't follow the standard. Therefore, if, in our example with the robot, we decide to create some new instructions for the robot to remember that tell it how to "open" something. This is quite all right with the C++ compiler (since we wrote the instructions ourselves) but it may confuse others (and you) later since open ≠ Open to the compiler.

Comments in Programming

Most programming languages encourage the creation of commentary in the body of the source code. The programmer may insert comments about what is happening, why it is happening, and other issues for all to see. This greatly assists in the reading and analysis of the program, particularly when others are reading/analyzing the code.

RealWorld

In the real world, organizations often have specific commenting requirements that programmers must use for consistency. Comments may link the lines of code to informational tools or plans such as flowcharts, data flow diagrams, and pseudocodes. Many comments in your programs will be helpful to your systems analyst and make your code easier to integrate with others'. Although there are certainly real-world programmers who use little or no commentary in their programs, unless you are a solo coder, you will find a real need for comments, if not a requirement.

Real-world programmers often work on many projects simultaneously and may have to switch from one project to another. Sometimes, programmers must return to work supposedly completed months or even years earlier. You will find that in this environment you need to be able to "get into" the code quickly and cannot spend days trying to remember what you were doing and why you were doing it. Commentary is often your only guide.

Properly designated commentary is ignored by the compiler, allowing the programmer to write comments in plain English or any other language/structure he or she wishes. This is a very useful tool for making source code readable. When a comment symbol is detected by the compiler, the compiler ignores the commentary and no errors are generated.

C++ provides for commentary in the form of both **in-line comments** and **block comments**. In addition, **document comments** (usually just called "doc" comments) are also available.

Figure 2.1.

In-Line Comments

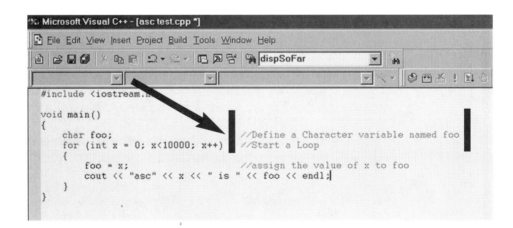

Figure 2.2

Block
Comments

```
#include <iostream.h>

/*******************************************************************
**                                                               **
**                                                               **
**   Programme:  ASCII Display programme                         **
**   Programmer: Doug White                                      **
**                                                               **
**   Simple programme to display all the decimal codes for all   **
**   of the ASCII and extended ASC char sets.                    **
**                                                               **
**                                                               **
*******************************************************************/

void main()
{
    char foo;                     //Define a Character variable named foo
    for (int x = 0; x<10000; x++)   //Start a Loop
    {
        foo = x;                  //assign the value of x to foo
        cout << "asc" << x << " is " << foo << endl;
    }
}
```

Definition 2.1
....

In-line comments are included on a line of source code. These comments are usually used to describe in English what a specific instruction in C++ is intended to do.

Definition 2.2
....

Block comments are long sections that appear at the beginning and in other key locations of the source code. This type of commentary usually provides documentation
of various structures, explanations of what is supposed to happen, information on
how to utilize the source code in different situations, references to flowcharts or
other planning materials, and/or general information about the program.

Definition 2.3
....

Doc Comments are designed to be extracted by other programs for use in the creation
of documentation for code to be published separately. Visual C++ supports this feature and this type of commentary is expected to gain in popularity as more source codes
are shared and reused within a company. Doc comments allow a file of documentation to be generated in a consistent manner.

In Visual C++, in-line comments are created by using the // symbols together. This
informs the compiler to ignore the rest of a physical line. The symbol /* is used together with
*/ to create a block comment in which everything contained within the block is ignored.

Scope Delimiters

Most programming languages have **scope delimiters**.

Definition 2.4

A *scope delimiter* is a symbol or pair of symbols used to define a region or area, which is considered a locale. For instance, in the real world, many states in the US used rivers or other natural features as boundaries for that state's scope. In programming, many structures need to have their scope defined because they should not affect the entire program. Thus, symbols are used to define scopes in pairs.

In C++, the symbols { and } are used as scope delimiters. These rarely used symbols became popular with the advent of C, which used them as well. It is important that you understand there is a difference between { } (curly braces or braces), ( ) (parentheses), and [ ] (square brackets or brackets). They are not equivalent and have different ASCII numbers. Your text will include detailed descriptions of where and how these delimiters are used in C++ programs.

Literals

Most programming languages allow programmers to use **literals.**

Definition 2.5

Literals are system commands or other pieces of information that the compiler doesn't really understand. Compilers are written to serve as general-purpose tools and often run on many different operating systems. This means that if the programmer has some specific instruction for the user or the operating system, it may be that the operating system's rule set (syntax) must be used instead. As the compiler can't possibly know all rule sets, these items are classified as literals by the compiler and special instructions are used to manage them.

In C++, literals are enclosed in " " (quotes), which tells the compiler that this is something to do with the operating system or with the user and a different set of rules applies. The most common use of this type of literal is to manage files in an operating system. While Visual C++ was designed to run in WINXX, you may notice from the listing of C++ compilers that many other operating systems are supported as well. If the programmer needs a file in VAX/VMS or MVS, the instructions for getting it may differ wildly from the commands used in WINXX. Even instructions specific to the WINXX operating system may not be supported by the Visual C++ compiler (for example, **C:/cppFun/myCPP.cpp**) since the operating system has an entirely different set of commands and keywords.

In C++ and other ASCII-based editors, there is no end quote so all quotes used are the same straight quote, for beginning and end. In modern word processing, however, reverse quotes are often used and I have had students ask where to find " on the keyboard. There is no standard ASCII number for this symbol, and it is not used in C++ programming. Always use the keyboard " (shift-apostrophe) for all quote usage in C++ source code. This is another good reason to use the environment editor or a text editor rather than a word processing program to create source code.

Example 2.1

Revisit our robot and consider the following instruction:
Say hello to our guest in Mandarin Chinese
你好

Now, as you might guess, the robot has no idea what these symbols mean but an instruction such as:
Display "你好" to our guest
may be carried out even if the robot has no idea why or what it is saying.

Columns and White Space in C++

For many years, programming was very structured, as it had evolved from the use of punched cards, which were based on columns. The COBOL, FORTRAN, and RPG programming languages all used punched cards in the 1960s and 1970s as a means of generating lines of source code (one line per card) and the cards were all based on everything being in certain columns. Some languages, such as RPG III, were extremely column oriented and required great care in the development of source code.

As you may guess, this was very tedious for programmers because they had to manage the columns and be very accurate with their placement of instructions or risk complaints from the compiler. Modern programming languages, for the most part, have gone to "free form" rules that use **delimiters** instead of columns to determine the end of instructions.

Definition 2.6

A *delimiter* is a symbol that terminates an instruction or set of instructions. In the English language a period (.) is used as a delimiter so that readers of English can still make sense of

"A   lot   of
spacing   and line   feeds   are used
here   to   make   a
point."

In C++, the delimiter used is a semi-colon (;). C++ doesn't really care about columns and the amount of "white space" used in a line of C++ source code. There are certainly conventions that we will discuss for formatting C++ source code, but as far the compiler is concerned, all of the source code could appear on one gigantic line. This would certainly make the programmer's job of editing difficult and would likely result in violence on the part of a systems analyst or instructor, though the compiler would be perfectly happy.

Most modern programmers tend to use indents (tabs), blank lines, and other strategies to make their programs more readable. There are "spaghetti coders" who write confused, complicated, programs that nevertheless work, but you should not follow their examples.

Indentation Conventions and Subordination

With the advent of free-form programming, came the use of indentation in source code. Most real-world programmers work in teams or at very least must submit portions of their code for approval from time to time. (This of course excludes gonzo, underground, game programmers who live in someone's basement, eat nothing but refried beans and Cheetos, and hope for a break into the big time someday.) Thus, programmers attempt to make their code easily legible by using white space and tabs.

Many programming instructions become subordinate to other instructions due to scope or other restrictions. Formatting the code to reflect this subordination helps the reader of the code understand its inherent logic.

Example 2.2

Let's assume we have another command for our robot. This command says "if," allowing the robot to make a clear choice based on some criteria. So, we can say:

If the user chooses Chinese as a language, then display " 你好"
Otherwise, display "Hello"

In the example, the display command is subordinate to the condition required to obtain that display so we might write the instructions using indents (tabs) to indicate clearly these conditional responses, for example:

If Chinese
  Display " 你好"
Otherwise
  Display "Hello"

This type of indentation allows the programmer (and others) to spot subordination in the program quickly and may help later in the understanding of problems that emerge due to misuse of subordination. It is worth noting that C++ does not care about this use of white space and would be satisfied with the following:

If Chinese Display " 你好" Otherwise Display "Hello"

Example 2.3

The following segment of C++ source code illustrates the use of comments, indentations, and white space:

```
#include <iostream.h>

/*********************************************************************
**                                                                 **
**                                                                 **
**   Program:   ASCII Display program                              **
**   Programmer:      Doug White                                   **
**                                                                 **
**   Simple program to display all the decimal codes for all       **
```

```
**   of the ASCII and extended ASC char sets. The program          **
**   runs through all the numbers in a loop and prints the          **
**   number and the ASC character on the screen.                    **
**                                                                  **
**                                                                  **
*************************************************************************/
void main()
{
    char foo;                   //Define a Character variable named foo
    for (int x = 0; x<10000; x++)     //Start a Loop
    {
        foo = x;                //assign the value of x to foo

        cout << "asc" << x << " is " << foo << endl;
    }
}
```

Case Conventions in C++

The most common practice among C++ programmers is to use small letters for the first part of a variable name and a capital letter to begin the second part.

Example 2.4

*If you create a name in C++ (called a **variable** or **identifier**) that will be used to hold some information about weight, you might name that variable theWeight using this popular naming convention.*

This convention is widely followed for most names the programmer creates in her source code. This helps programmers avoid using keywords (remember they are all lower case) as names. The same convention is also used in the Java, Visual Basic, and C programming languages and has become a standard for programming.

RealWorld   Remember that programmers often do unusual things and fail to follow convention. Companies also make their own conventions for their own reasons so you may encounter many programs in the real world that have very different standards.

Hungarian Notation

Hungarian notation is an approach to defining names in programming in which a descriptive prefix is attached to a given variable name. As with any convention, there are many variants and many who ignore it completely. Essentially, Hungarian notation involves the attempt to identify a variable by its type and use in the program. For instance, a signed integer variable might be named **iMyInt** in C++ using Hungarian notation. A float might be described as **fMyFloat**. Your instructor may or may not wish to discuss this type of notation in your course.

Color Coding in Visual C++

If you use the Visual C++ editor to develop your source codes, you will find that the editor does everything it can to assist you in developing error-free code. One of the ways it does this is through automatic color-coding for all the ANSI standard components of C++.

Comments

All comments (both block and in-line) in C++ will appear color-coded in green to indicate that these instructions are considered commentary by the compiler and are being ignored. In Figure 2.3 we see several types of comments displayed on the screen by the C++ editor. (**NOTE:** The text in the book does not appear in color, but these comments in the Visual Studio development environment will appear in green as indicated.)

Figure 2.3

Two Types of Comments

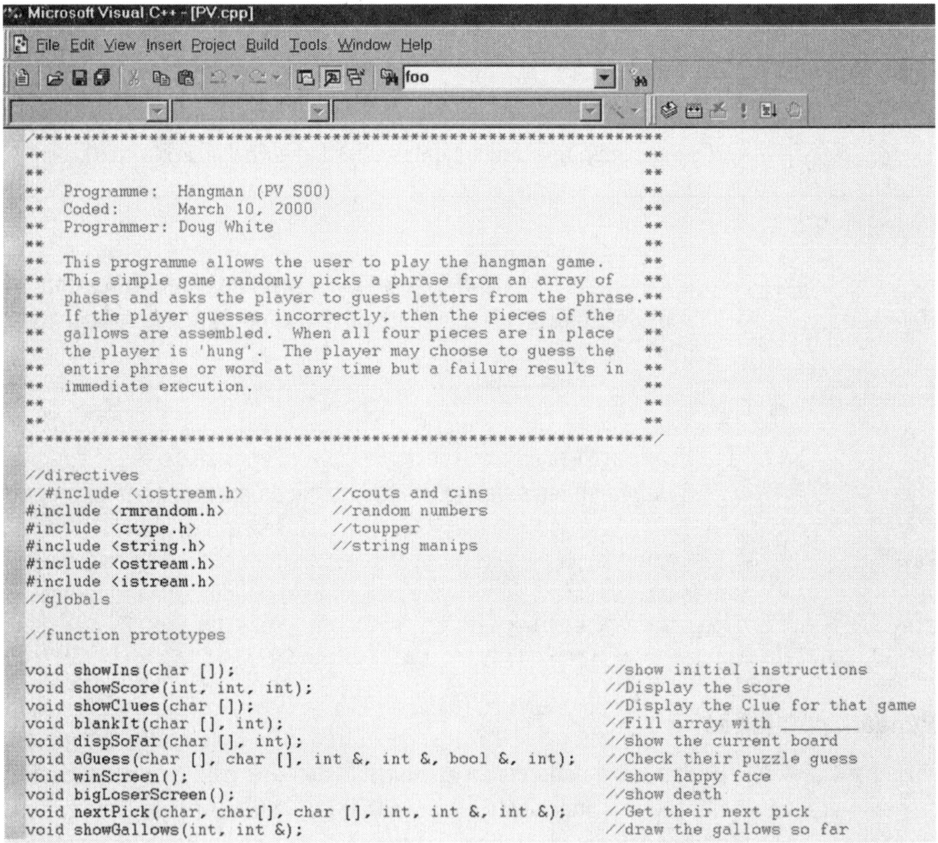


```
/*****************************************************************
**                                                              **
**                                                              **
**  Programme:  Hangman (PV S00)                                **
**  Coded:      March 10, 2000                                  **
**  Programmer: Doug White                                      **
**                                                              **
**  This programme allows the user to play the hangman game.    **
**  This simple game randomly picks a phrase from an array of   **
**  phases and asks the player to guess letters from the phrase.**
**  If the player guesses incorrectly, then the pieces of the   **
**  gallows are assembled.  When all four pieces are in place   **
**  the player is 'hung'.  The player may choose to guess the   **
**  entire phrase or word at any time but a failure results in  **
**  immediate execution.                                        **
**                                                              **
**                                                              **
*****************************************************************/

//directives
//#include <iostream.h>         //couts and cins
#include <rmrandom.h>           //random numbers
#include <ctype.h>              //toupper
#include <string.h>             //string manips
#include <ostream.h>
#include <istream.h>
//globals

//function prototypes

void showIns(char []);                                      //show initial instructions
void showScore(int, int, int);                              //Display the score
void showClues(char []);                                    //Display the Clue for that game
void blankIt(char [], int);                                 //Fill array with ______
void dispSoFar(char [], int);                               //show the current board
void aGuess(char [], char [], int &, int &, bool &, int);   //Check their puzzle guess
void winScreen();                                           //show happy face
void bigLoserScreen();                                      //show death
void nextPick(char, char[], char [], int, int &, int &);    //Get their next pick
void showGallows(int, int &);                               //draw the gallows so far
```

In this example notice that the programmer has used block comments (starting with /*) at the top of the program to describe the program and then used in-line comments throughout this listing to identify various structures in the C++ program. Notice that on the in-line comments, only the comment (the part ignored by the C++ processor) will be shown in green.

NOTE: It is possible to accidentally create comments where they were unexpected. In Figure 2.4, a programmer has forgotten to terminate his block commentary with */ and now he essentially has no source code as it is all ignored by the compiler.

The programmer should always take note of green comment code and make sure that comments are only where the programmer expected them to be and not affecting the rest of the source code in any way. There is more discussion on this in the section on debugging.

Figure 2.4

Comment Errors

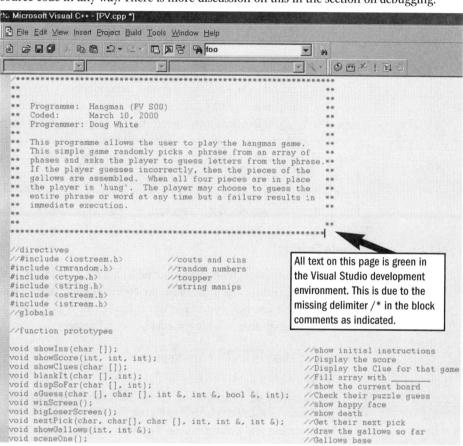

Keywords

All ANSI keywords in C++ are coded in blue. You can use this feature to spot the proper and improper use of keywords. For instance, examining the screen shown in Figure 2.5, you notice that the same keyword (include) is blue in two instances and black in another (indicated by the highlight here). See if you can spot the reason for this difference.

Figure 2.5

Keywords

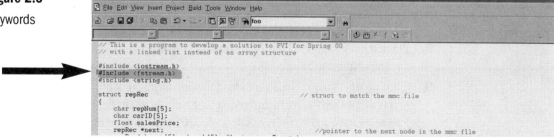

The difference is that the second indicated keyword **#Include** is capitalized by mistake. This causes the compiler to fail to recognize **#Include** as a keyword. Remember that Include ≠ include in C++ and that all the ANSI keywords in C++ are lowercase. After you use the editor for a bit you will quickly take note when you type in a keyword and it doesn't turn blue. The bad news is, after you get used to this system, it is hard to use a non-environment type editor since you are constantly wondering why the color didn't change.

Non-ANSI Keywords

One point to note about C++ is that there are many additional non-ANSI keywords in frequent use. The compiler has no idea what these keywords are and, therefore, these keywords will not appear in blue. Just like names you create, names created by other programmers and used by you are considered "other" by the compiler and will always appear in plain black type. Two very commonly used keywords in this category are **cin** and **cout**. These non-ANSI keywords are added in by programmers when they want to do input and output to the screen. Unless at some future date they are added to the ANSI standard, they will always appear in black typeface because the compiler doesn't recognize them as standard keywords.

Creating Source Code Tutorial
· · · · · · · · · · · · · · · ·

You now have enough information to type in a source code file. At this point, we want to walk through creating a new file of source code and then typing a simple program into the editor. We won't run the program in this tutorial. (All references to the "Explorer" denote the **Windows Explorer**, not the Internet browser, Explorer.)

Setting up the Visual C++ Workspace

1. If you installed the Visual C++ disk successfully in Chapter 1, then you should be able to run it from the **Start** menu. Left-click the mouse on the **Start** button in the lower left corner of your screen seen in Figure 2.6. This should allow you to bring up a list of the programs and utilities installed on your system similar to that shown in the left menu column of Figure 2.7

Figure 2.6

The Start Button

2. Move the mouse onto the Programs section and a list of all the different subdirectories of programs will appear. This may say Visual Studio (as in the middle menu column of Figure 2.7) or it may say Visual C++. Visual C++ is a component of Visual Studio or a stand-alone program, depending on what you have purchased. If you are using the bundle that came with the book, you should see Visual C++ 6.0, as shown in the far right menu column of Figure 2.7.

3. Left-click on the **Visual C++** icon to load the environment. When the load is complete, you should see the main environment screen shown in Figure 2.8. This is an empty workplace. You should verify that you are in Visual C++ by looking in the

upper left corner of the program as shown in Figure 2.9—an enlargement of the top of 2.8. (Several other applications, including Visual Basic, look very similar to Visual C++.)

Figure 2.7

The Programs Section leading to Visual Studio and finally to The Visual C++ Icon

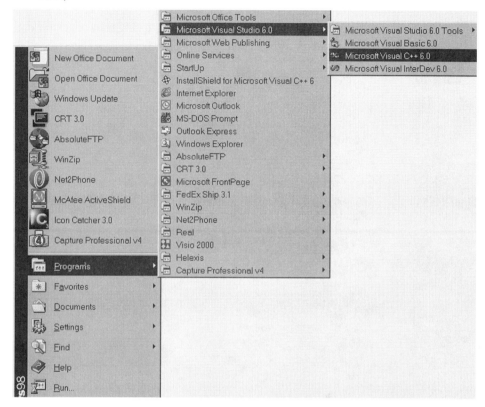

Figure 2.8

The Visual C++ Work Environment

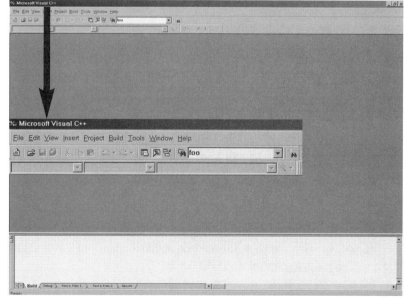

Figure 2.9

The Visual C++ Verify

4. As with any Microsoft product, you may create a new work area by choosing the **File** menu and **New** shown in Figure 2.10. This provides you with the menu shown in Figure 2.11.

   The menu may be quite confusing due to the sheer volume of file types, project workspaces, and so forth. For now, we are only interested in examining the source code in a single file option. Later, we will explore other options from this menu.

Figure 2.10

The New Menu Item

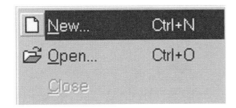

Figure 2.11

The Main New File Screen

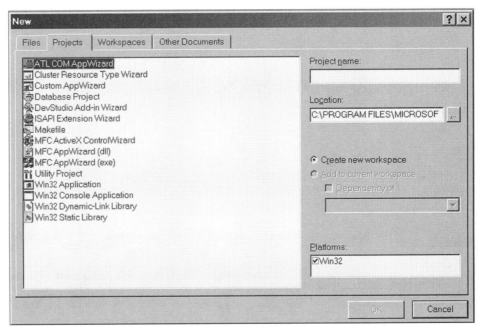

Figure 2.12

The Files Tab

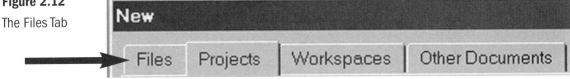

5. Now, you need to click the **Files** tab at the top of the screen as shown in Figure 2.12. This provides you with another daunting set of options, as shown in Figure 2.13.

6. Now, select the **C++ Source File** option as shown in Figure 2.14, which will allow you to reach the editor.

Figure 2.13

The Files Options

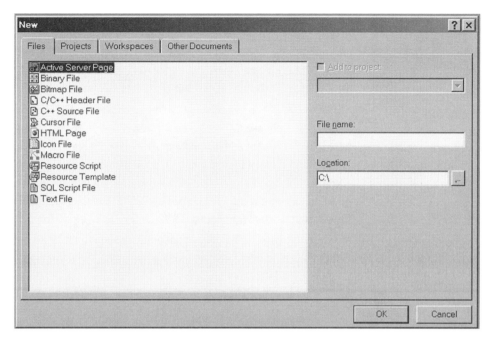

Figure 2.14

The C++ Source
File Option

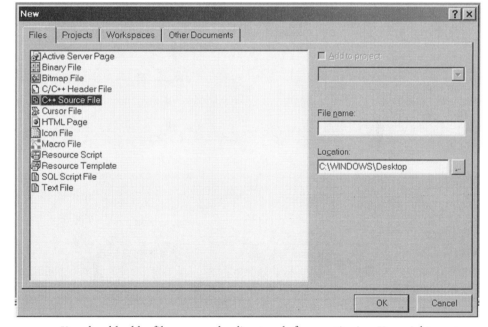

You should add a filename and a directory before continuing. You might create a separate subdirectory on your hard drive, Zip disk, or floppy disk. For this exercise, let's create a directory on the C: drive (you might be using a different drive, so use whatever letter is appropriate) called **cppFun** and we will name this first program, **myFirstCpp**.

Figure 2.15

The Windows Key

7. The directory doesn't exist; so first create it by using the **Windows** key and **e** (press the two keys together) to start the Windows Explorer. The **Windows** key is shown in Figure 2.15. Your keyboard may not have a **Windows** key if it is an older computer or keyboard. In this case, just right-click on the **Start** button and choose **Explore** to run the Explorer as you see in Figure 2.16. Either way, you should see the Explorer window shown in Figure 2.17.

8. At this point, choose the drive you are interested in using, (shown here is the **C:** hard drive) and double left-click the drive letter. This will show you all the subdirectories that exist currently on that drive as in Figure 2.18.

9. If you wish to use an existing directory, you may, but the following steps show you how to create a new one called **cppFun** on the C: drive. Choose the **File** menu then **New Folder** as shown in Figure 2.19.

10. After you left-click on **Folder**, you should see something like what is highlighted in Figure 2.20.

Figure 2.16

The Right-Click on Start

Figure 2.17

The Explorer

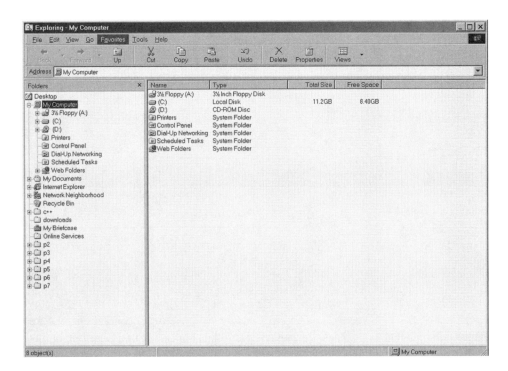

Figure 2.18

Subdirectories on
Drive C:

Figure 2.19

Creating a New
Subdirectory
(New/Folder)

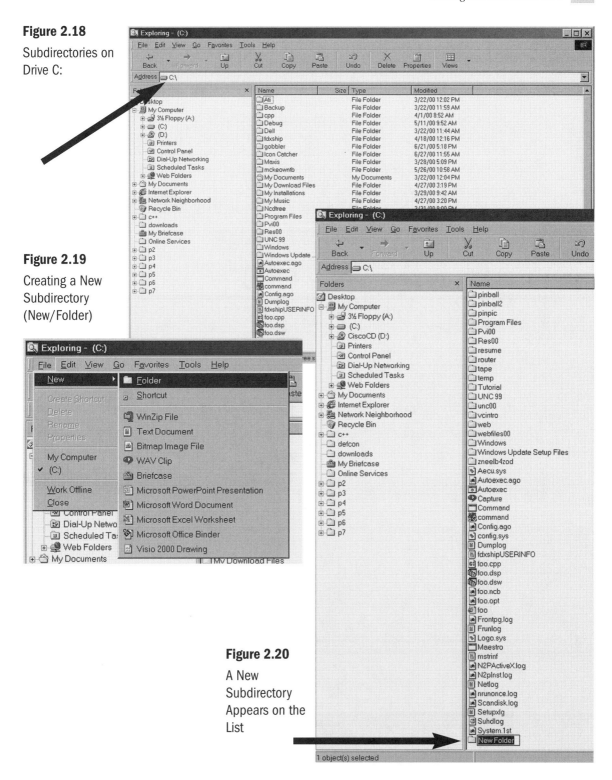

Figure 2.20

A New
Subdirectory
Appears on the
List

11. Change the **NewFolder** name to **cppFun**, as shown in Figure 2.21, by typing it in and pressing **Enter**. NOTE: Your screen will look different from the example because you have a different disk structure than the one in the sample, but the folder itself should look the same.

12. You can close the Explorer now by clicking on the **X** button in the upper right hand corner of the screen as shown in Figure 2.22.

13. Now, we'll go back to Visual C++ and create our file. You should type the name **myFirstCpp** in the File name box and the disk drive you are using (**X:**, substitute the appropriate drive letter, for **X** on your machine) and the subdirectory **cppFun** in the location box as shown in Figure 2.23.

14. Click the **OK** button and you should see the Main Edit screen shown in Figure 2.24.

Figure 2.21

Naming the cppFun Subdirectory

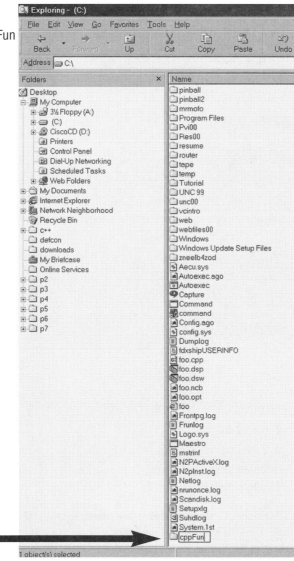

Figure 2.22

The X Button

Figure 2.23

Creating the
Empty
myFirstCpp
File

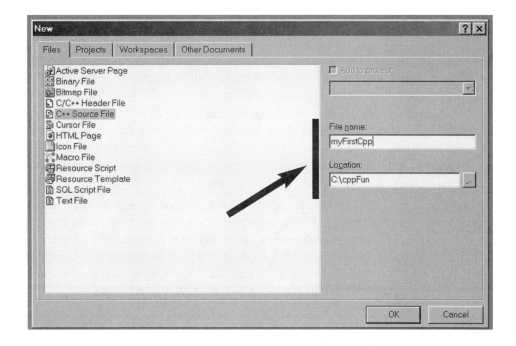

Figure 2.24

The Main Edit
Screen

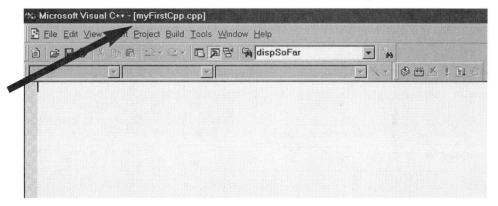

You can see the name of your file in the upper left hand corner with the directory and sub-directory.

InfoBox

You should always use subdirectories to store your files. Visual C++ creates quite a few work files when it generates the executable file for your source code, and they will be easy to dispose of if you keep everything together in one convenient place. Under no circumstances should you use the root (C:\) directory except on a floppy disk (which is small enough that not too much clutter can accumulate. Using subdirectories is wise even on floppy disks because you can organize all your files much easier that way.

Entering the Source Code

15. You can begin typing in source code and commentary here in the edit window and continue until you are finished. Save your work often because there is no autosave in Visual C++. If there is a power failure or other problem, you may lose all your typing.

    One interesting feature of the Visual C++ editor is the intelligent indentation and pair matching of scope delimiters. The editor will attempt to line up all the code for you if you will let it. So, when you are typing the sample program into the editor, take note of how the editor indents the code. It usually knows what it is doing. With minor exceptions, the layout of the lines and whitespace will not matter to the compiler, but try to reproduce the program below.

    In the following example, you should type **exactly** the source code that is given, paying particular attention to the case of the example. Your instructor may wish to give you a different sample program to enter here. This simple example doesn't make use of the structured approach to programming. It might be called "spaghetti code" by experienced programmers. Nevertheless, it is easy to type and provides good practice for beginning programmers in getting the code in place.

Example 2.5

Source Listing for Birthstone Program

```
/************************************************************************
**                                                                    **
**   Program:   Example Exercise 2.5 from Visual C++ Text             **
**   Programmer:        Doug White                                     **
**   Date:              June 27, 2000                                  **
**                                                                    **
**   This is a very simple program to provide a first program         **
**   experience for beginning programmers in Visual C++ 6.0.          **
**   The program asks the user for their birthday month and then      **
**   determines their birthstone based the month they were            **
**   born.                                                             **
**                                                                    **
************************************************************************/

#include <iostream.h>                          //standard io file
#include <ctype.h>

void main()
{
    //Main program

    int aMonth = 0;
    bool anAlien = false;
    char resp = 'N';

    do {

        cout << "What numerical month were you born (1-12)?" << endl;
```

```
cin >> aMonth;

switch (aMonth)                              //test the data
{
case 1:
{
     cout << "Garnet ";
     break;
}
case 2:
{
     cout << "Amethyst ";
     break;
}
case 3:
{
     cout << "Aquamarine ";
     break;
}
case 4:
{
     cout << "Diamond ";
     break;
}
case 5:
{
     cout << "Emerald ";
     break;
}
case 6:
{
     cout << "Pearl ";
     break;
}
case 7:
{
     cout << "Ruby ";
     break;
}
case 8:
{
     cout << "Sardonyx ";
     break;
}
case 9:
{
     cout << "Sapphire ";
     break;
}
case 10:
{
     cout << "Opal ";
```

(Continued)

```
                        break;
                    }
                    case 11:
                    {
                        cout << "Topaz ";
                        break;
                    }
                    case 12:
                    {
                        cout << "Turquoise ";
                        break;
                    }
                    default:
                    {
                        //something is wrong
                        cout << "Sorry, Earth months only" << endl;
                        anAlien = true;
                        break;
                    }
                }   //end switch

                if (!anAlien)
                {
                    cout << "is your birthstone!" << endl;
                    cout << "Do another? (Y/N)" << endl;
                    cin >> resp;
                }
            }while (toupper(resp) = 'Y');
        }
//the end
```

16. When you have finished with the source code, you should save your file by choosing **File** then **Save** as shown in Figure 2.25. This completes the exercise for inputting source code. Go back and take careful note of the keywords, the commentary, and the white space in the program for future reference.

Figure 2.25

The File Save Function

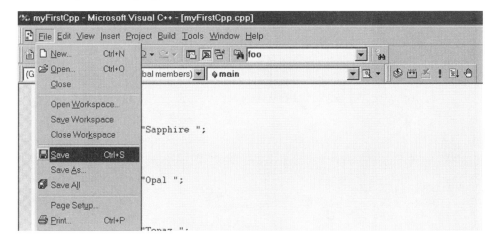

Running this Program (optional)

You may want to run the program you have just entered. You should be prepared for it to contain errors, which may seem discouraging at this point. A suggestion is that you wait until you have finished the debugging tutorials in Chapter 3 to run this program. However, if you really want to run the source code you just created, just add these steps to the tutorial (or use the Chapter 3 tutorial for more detail).

1. Press the **Rebuild All** button. See Figure 2.26. If the program compiles successfully (no errors), you will see a screen similar to Figure 2.27.

Figure 2.26

The Rebuild All Button

Figure 2.27

The Successful Compile

Figure 2.28

The Run or
Execute Button

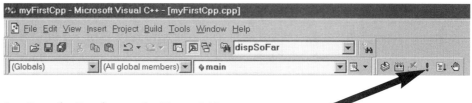

2.   Press the **Run** button. See Figure 2.28.

Again, if the program contains errors, just wait until you have completed the
debugging tutorials, come back, and get some debugging practice.

Saving and Managing Source Code Files

In an educational setting, as in the real world, it may prove necessary to develop a method
for managing files to keep up with all the programs you write. Companies usually have a
file management and protection system. This section discusses protecting your work, managing
files, and some useful approaches to development found in the real world.

File Naming and Version Management

Everyone comes up with schema for naming things. Often these are not very useful and end
up adding to the confusion when you forget the clever approach you designed years ago. For
instance, in the author's archive is a file called 101197phil.cob. It's a COBOL file and the
numbers probably indicate a date. "Phil" is a former boss, so perhaps it has something to do
with him. Beyond that, there are no clues to its purpose.

As you start developing your own programs, you will find is the need to maintain both
backup copies and older versions of the code. Sometimes programmers, especially beginning
programmers, make changes that are not necessarily the best. Their code gets so convoluted
that they cannot sort it out and need to return to a previous version. Use the method common
in the industry, version-numbering. Admittedly, this means you have multiple copies of the program on your disk, but since most educational software is not that large and in industry, you
should have plenty of storage space available, it's a good approach.

Software developers use a numbering system with multiple parts to describe the changes
that have taken place between versions. The numbers commonly look something like 6.7.8.9.
For our purposes let's just propose you maintain three files. Call them A, B, and C. In the
industry, the first number from the left is used to describe the main version number and
changes here represent total revisions of the program (so that Windows98 Version 1.0 is usually drastically different from Version 2.0) such that **backwards compatibility** becomes an
issue.

Definition 2.6

Backwards compatibility refers to the ability of a new version of an application to
work with files created by an older version of the application. An example would be Visual
C++ 6.0 being able to process files created with Visual C++ 5.0. (**NOTE:** As a rule, there
is no "forwards compatibility.")

Each number you move to the right represents change at a lower and lower level of the code such that a change from 6.7.8.9 to 6.7.8.10 might represent only a minor modification affecting a tiny number of code users.

Students should keep the three copies and use them as a version development approach. Assign the working file a name such as PIIIsp00.cpp for assignment 3 in Spring of 2000. When a milestone is accomplished that is worth saving (for example, the first draft of the source code), save an extra copy as PIIIA.cpp in the same directory. You could return to this milestone if large-scale problems result when working on the source code later. The next time a milestone is accomplished, save the file as PIIIB.cpp and now, essentially, two copies of the program exist at different points in time. If the programmer really needed to, he or she could go back to A and start over from that point without too much trouble. PIIIC.cpp represents another milestone. Usually just keep using the letters of the alphabet, and in academic development, you won't run out of letters. After a while, if you are having space limitation problems, you may want to delete some early versions of the code.

You can certainly extend this in more complex projects to names such as A1 or B27 to distinguish minor milestones as well as major milestones. This can save you a lot of work if you really get things muddled at three o'clock in the morning in the computer lab, not to mention the comfort of being able to return to a previous milestone instead of starting all over if you lose a file. Your instructor likely has some horror stories of lost files and late-night errors to share and may wish to specify her preferred approaches to file naming.

Disk Space Issues

Obviously, the best solution to disk space problems is to run Visual C++ on a hard disk drive that is large and almost empty. This is not available to most people, but it is certainly the best solution. You are left with a number of storage choices:

- Hard Disk Drive
- Floppy Disk Drive
- Zip Disk
- CD-Rom Drive

You will find that source code and text files in general are quite small, usually insignificant in terms of the gigantic hard drives available today. Even a one-megabyte floppy disk is large by text file standards.

The only real issue you will face is the storage of the secondary files for all the programs as they are created by Visual C++. Visual C++ creates six files for each program and some of these files can be two or three times the size of the source code file. Students usually run out of disk space on a floppy disk quite rapidly. Therefore, consider using a Zip disk or a different floppy disk for each project. As CD-Rom burners become commonplace, they offer another option.

The only downside to having all your projects on your hard disk at home is that you may find you need the disk available at school, and it's just a good idea to have it with you. If for example, you drop by your instructor's office to report, "I think I am done," and she says,

"How did you deal with the array?" and you think, "What array? There was an array needed?" You will find it convenient to have your materials with you so you can modify your array.

In addition, you can delete any of the files except the source code files (**.cpp**) in your directory because they are all created by the compiler and can be recreated any time you wish simply by recompiling. The compiler will also create a "debug" folder that contains additional files and the **.exe** file for your program. These two can also be deleted and recreated as required.

Finally, remember that you will have problems with Visual C++ if you are out of disk space or even low on disk space (say 95 percent of the disk is full). This condition may cause your program to fail, Visual C++ to crash, or frustrating errors during the compile process. Thus, you should always be aware of the amount of disk space available to you, especially if you are in a lab.

If you want to check the disk space on a WinXX machine, do the following:

1. Press the **Windows** and **e** key simultaneously. You should see something similar to Figure 2.29.

2. Next, left-click on the device you want to check. Its capacity and free space will appear at the bottom of the window. See Figure 2.30. (You may also right-click the device and choose **Properties** for a more in-depth examination of the device.)

This figure shows an 11.25-gigabyte drive with 8.35 gigabytes free. The user wouldn't have to worry. The project tutorial you completed earlier shows how much space a simple project in Visual C++ might take up. If you open the **cppFun** directory we created earlier, you should be able to see the size of the file you typed. Later, when we compile the files, you can check the size of the entire directory.

Figure 2.29

The Explorer Screen

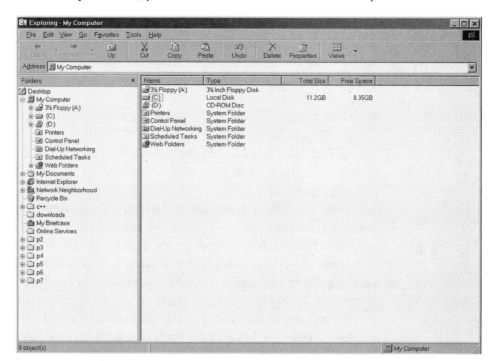

Figure 2.30

The Disk Space
Available

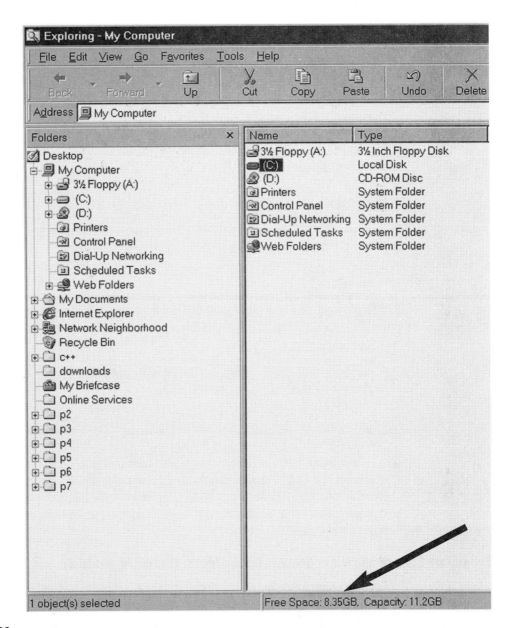

Backup Copies

It is vital that you make backup copies of your work. All storage media are subject to failures, and the failures usually occur at inopportune moments, such as the day an assignment is due.

Hard disks and even CDs are not immune to failure. You should always make backup copies, even though it will cost additional time before you can go home. Don't be the student who shows his instructor a 3.5-inch floppy disk that looks like a fried egg and asks, "It got really hot in my car and all my term projects are on this disk. Do you think you can get them back?" The answer is "No."

If you are storing the files on a floppy disk, then duplicate the disk on another floppy and make a copy on the hard drive of the machine if it's your machine. This makes several copies on different media. The same goes for a Zip disk or a CD. Make sure you have at least one extra copy of the file on a different media. Name the files something with the extension .bak so that you can remember that they are backup files. If you need to restore them later, you can rename them.

One very important point to remember about backing up files on hard disks is that many labs and home computers are set up with **partitions** on the **physical drive** to create multiple **logical drives**.

Definition 2.7

A *partition* is a means of creating a barrier on a storage device such that separate drive letters may be assigned to each partition, (for example, C:, D:, E:).

Definition 2.8

A *physical drive* is a single drive unit such as a hard disk, a CD, or a floppy drive.

Definition 2.9

A *logical drive* is a drive that is contained in a physical device. Thus, many logical drives may share a single physical drive.

The danger is that if the physical drive fails, all of the logical drives on that device may also fail. Therefore, you should try to keep your source code files on separate media.

In addition, you need to protect these backup copies of the media. If a backup copy is left in a drive, it might be stolen along with the computer. Identify some safe place and keep your backup copies all together there. In commercial applications, you might consider off-site storage of files, but in academic work, simply making a separate copy on a different media is usually sufficient.

Laboratory Storage and Other Security Issues for Programming Students

Computer labs are notorious locations for security problems. Everyone from expert hackers down to novice programmers uses the facility, often at the same time. Several categories of problems manifest themselves when you are using any machine that is available to the public:

- Viruses
- Plagiarism
- Theft
- Malicious Mischief

Viruses

Computer viruses are virtually uncountable. If you look at some of the commercial anti-virus products, you will see literally hundreds of thousands of known virus definitions, let alone all the yet undiscovered viruses running around. It takes only seconds to install a virus (often unwittingly) on a machine. Lab machines are notorious for having viruses because so many different people are running software and disks through them.

If you are transporting disks between home and school, you should have anti-virus software in place. Scan any disks you are taking home before you leave the lab. This will help ensure that you spread no viruses. You should also have anti-virus software in place on your home machine (or anywhere else you use these disks). Not all viruses are known and the anti-virus software in your lab may be dated or not working properly.

If you are e-mailing files back and forth or sharing them via the web, the cautions also apply. Many viruses can be transported via e-mail or attached to files. In addition, you need to make sure the anti-virus software you are using contains the most current virus information. Many people install the software and then never update it. Whatever software you are using should have a website containing regular updates and instructions on how to use them. Commercial providers of anti-virus software are Symantec (www.symantec.com), McAffee (www.mcaffee.com), and Computer Associates (www.ca.com). If you don't have anti-virus protection, you will have problems eventually.

Plagiarism

A second issue is plagiarism. Sadly, many people are too lazy to do their own work. Cheating happens. You need to protect your work, as there are sure to be some people who would rather steal your programs than learn how to make their own. If they are caught, they may not admit to the act but instead turn and accuse you. People get copies of others' work in several key ways:

- Shoulder Surfing

- Temp Directories

- Shared Directories

- Discarded Print

- New Print

Shoulder surfing is as old as Programming 101 and involves persons wandering around the lab looking for "help" on their programs.

Temp directories are often placed on lab machines so that students can store their work temporarily. Most students neglect to delete their files from these directories when they are finished working. Lab administrators or automated processes will eventually delete the files, but sometimes these directories are shared over a network! Cheaters will often cruise machines not in use, surfing for files such as CS1610PIII.cpp (or whatever) so that they can use or sell to others. If you are using temp directories on the lab machines, be sure to use generic names (like oldwork.tmp) and delete your files when you are done using the machine. This will prevent others from finding your programs and copying them. You might even password protect the files.

Sometimes, the temp or other directories used for public storage are shared across the lab. This is an open invitation for someone to either copy your files or just watch you do the work and then copy your changes. You should never use these directories when working on programming projects. Other persons can simply take your work without your even knowing it was stolen. You may want to check with your lab administrator or instructor if you are unsure about the status of a public directory on the lab machine.

One of the oldest rackets in the computer lab is the acquisition of printouts from either the trash or the public line printer. Take your old printouts home with you to toss in the recycle bin or at very least take them elsewhere in the building. Cheaters also prefer to pick up nice, new copies of assignments as they are printing out. The moral is to keep up with your work and make sure you are not providing someone an opportunity to get himself and you in hot water with your instructor, trying to explain who copied whom.

Theft

Computer labs are also locations ripe for your personal possessions to be stolen. If you are using Zip disks, be careful about leaving them in the drives. They can be carried away in a second with your hard-earned work on them.

Take great care with laptops, CDs, and other personal equipment you may be handling in the lab. If you walk away to get a printout, someone may simply walk away with your laptop. Thieves are also after your work and may take action to get it beyond simple plagiarism. Disks, laptops, CDs are often stolen just in pursuit of source code.

Malicious Mischief

Hackers and pranksters love to target novice users with harmless, and sometimes not so harmless, mischief. Any sort of suspicious actions you notice should be reported. Novice programmers often have their files erased or changed around by hackers in the lab. It is very frustrating when you have spent fifty hours developing an assignment and someone decides to delete the file for fun while you were out getting coffee. Always protect your files and keep them away from public access. Most people of the hacker persuasion prefer to target easy-access type files.

RealWorld

Learning to practice good security habits in college is useful preparation for the corporate environment where theft and mischief cost companies millions of dollars each year. Companies expend great effort and resources to protect their source code.

3

The Compiling and Debugging Process

You will find that creating the source code file is the simplest part of creating the application. The challenges start when you attempt to compile your source code (create the executable file) for the first time. If you are like most programmers, your source code will contain errors and other problems that you will have to fix before the executable can be created. You may find that even though you followed all the rules, you still have problems with the way the program operates. This chapter focuses on the conversion of your source code into an executable file. It also provides you with some exercises to get you started on this process.

Compiling Files

The Compile Process

Once you have created a source code file, then you can attempt to compile it into an object file. Most programmers, particularly, beginning programmers, will spend a great of time at this stage deciphering error messages and making corrections to source code. In the earlier chapters, we referred to the object file, which was created from the source code and resulted in a machine language file that could be "linked" into the library of C++ instructions. This is the first step in the process of compilation.

You need to save your source code. We will pick up at the end of the tutorial from Chapter 2 where we created the **myFirstCpp** file. This program should work, but you may have made typographical errors when you typed it into the editor and those typos will cause errors to happen when you compile the program. Let's walk through a quick compile so that you can see whether you were meticulous and typed the program exactly or made some minor mistakes. We'll use this experience as a guideline for our discussion of errors.

The easiest way to get back into the **myFirstCpp** program is to open the **cppFun** subdirectory and double left-click on the icon for the file **myFirstCpp**. When you open the subdirectory, you should see something like Figure 3.1.

If you don't see the file or were not able to type it in, you can copy it from the accompanying CD and use it here.

After you double left-click on the icon, Visual C++ should open and your source code appear in the main window as shown in Figure 3.2.

Scan the source code for obvious errors before attempting to compile the code the first time. This kind of proofreading helps you to avoid those long lists of errors so frustrating to beginning programmers. However, as you are just starting out, you may not recognize the errors initially. When you have a little more experience in your course, you should definitely make this a practice.

Figure 3.1

The cppFun Subdirectory

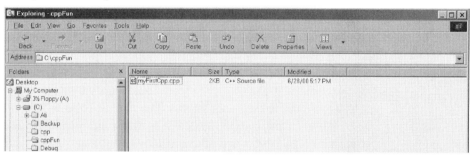

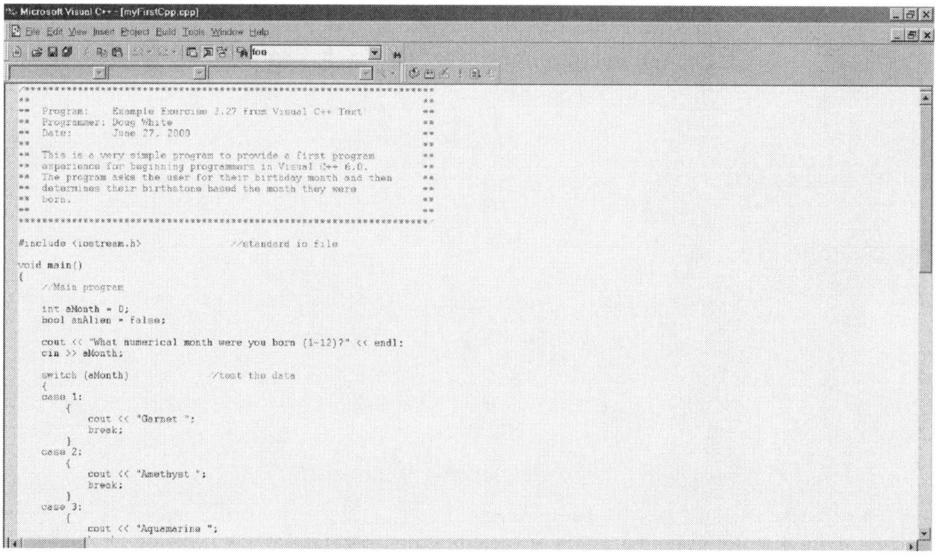

Figure 3.2

The Source Code in Visual C++

Figure 3.3

The Compile
Button

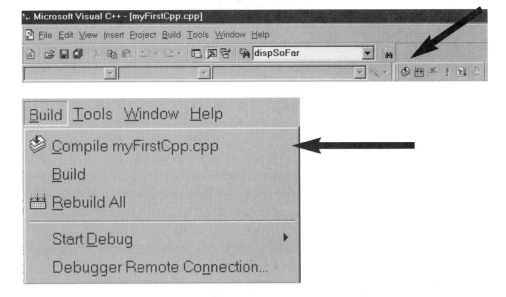

Figure 3.4

The Build Menu

Figure 3.5

The Default
Project
Workspace
Option

You should now attempt to create an object file from your source and see how well you did with the typing. There are several paths to this goal in Visual C++. The **Compile** button on the button bar will work, as will the first item on the **Build** menu. Use whichever you are more comfortable with and can remember. The button is depicted in Figure 3.3.

The **Build** menu also handles all the compilation tasks. If you open the **Build** menu, you will see some options that look like the ones shown in Figure 3.4.

This menu controls most every aspect of the compile process, so it's good to be familiar with its use. The first option on the menu **Compile myFirstCpp.cpp** allows you to send your source code to the compiler to have it processed. At this point you should either left-click on this option, or close the menu and click the **Compile** button. Visual C++ will then ask if you want to use a default project workspace (see Figure 3.5).

Choose **Yes**. A default work area will be created by Visual C++ and the files needed by the compiler will be placed in this area. Once you click **Yes**, the lower window will become active, and you will see the compile process taking place (Figure 3.6 on page 50).

This assumes you were successful in typing in the program exactly. You may be notified of a failure in the compile process due to errors in inputting the source code. Such a failure message is shown in Figure 3.7.

Figure 3.6

The Successful
Compile Process

```
-------------------Configuration: myFirstCpp - Win32 Debug--------------------
Compiling...
myFirstCpp.cpp

myFirstCpp.obj - 0 error(s), 0 warning(s)  ◀━━━━━━━━━━━━
```

Figure 3.7

The Unsuccessful
Compile Process

```
C:\cppFun\myFirstCpp.cpp(22) : error C2275: 'bool' : illegal use of this type as an expression
        c:\cppfun\myfirstcpp.cpp(0) : see declaration of 'bool'
C:\cppFun\myFirstCpp.cpp(22) : error C2065: 'anAlien' : undeclared identifier
C:\cppFun\myFirstCpp.cpp(24) : error C2146: syntax error : missing ';' before identifier 'cout'
Error executing cl.exe.

myFirstCpp.exe - 5 error(s), 0 warning(s)  ◀━━━━━━━━━━━━
```

In this example, the user has received five error messages and zero warning messages. This allows us to begin a discussion of these problems and how to approach correcting them.

Syntax and Logic Errors

All of the errors you deal with in programming fall in to two categories—**logic errors** and **syntax errors**. As beginning programmers, you will encounter many of each type. Learning to get rid of them is as much an art as it is a science. We may compare learning to program with learning to play a musical instrument. When you first start it's frustrating because you can't do even a simple song the instructor plays easily. The only solution is practice, practice, practice. Over time, you will develop shortcuts to solving problems and you will begin to develop strategies for approaching even the most complex issues. This is one of the reasons that programmers were traditionally required to take a lot of math. While you may never have take a dervative in real life, the process of working through a calculus problem is very similar to the process used to solve a programming problem.

Definition 3.1

A *syntax error* is simply a violation of the rules of a language. Much as the use of the word "ain't" is considered a violation of English syntax, the misuse of structure and form in programming is a violation of the compiler's rules. Both can result in missed communication and a halt in the process you desire.

When the initial compile takes place, the compiler carefully looks at each instruction in your code and compares it to what it knows and what has been defined by the programmer. For each instruction that is unknown, an error occurs. Beginning programmers encounter a great many syntax errors of this type since they are essentially writing in an unfamiliar language. This might equate to trying to write a paper in German or Spanish instead of your native language. Most of us make many grammatical and spelling errors in our own language; when we try another, the problem is even worse.

The more complicated problems begin when you are successful in compiling the source code and then the program doesn't behave as expected. This can be devastating if you are developing commercial applications. Your company would be very embarrassed when the product turns into a constant parade of calls from users wanting to know why **myFirstCpp** crashed again. Even worse would be the case of a program that doesn't do what was expected but continues to function.

This type of problem is called a logic error. Logic errors manifest themselves in strange ways. One of the oldest acronyms in computer science is GIGO, which stands for garbage in, garbage out. Programmers must be on guard to eliminate logic errors, as they will likely be to blame when the program results in catastrophe.

Definition 3.2

A *logic error* is a mistake that complies with the rules of the compiler. It may take the form of a misentered value, a mathematical expression that is coded incorrectly, or any other form. This type of error is very dangerous and is difficult to detect without a great deal of testing.

Unlike syntax errors, which are detected by the compiler, logic errors may go undetected until the program is processed using test data or, even worse, until the application is released! Later in this chapter, we will discuss some strategies for detecting logic errors during development.

Real World

Imagine that a programmer is writing a program to print payroll checks for hourly workers and one of the inputs the programmer uses is the hourly rate for a Type 7 employee (whatever that is). Now, suppose the wage should be input as $15.25 per hour, but instead the wage is input as $15.52 per hour, a common mistake called a transposition. Each week Bill, a Type 7 makes $620.80 instead of $610.00 if he works 40 hours. The problem may go unnoticed for a long time. After eight weeks, Bill would have been overpaid $86.40; after 52 weeks $561.60. Imagine the company has 700 Type 7 employees who are all overpaid for one year. A $393,120.00 deficit will be revealed when the books are audited and guess who will be to blame?

Another real world example would be the process of creating an application to compute the meters of steel needed to build a bridge across the Hudson River. Suppose an engineer uses the program. The calculation is off due to "rounding" or some other mathematical error. When the bridge is built, it fails to cross the river by 100 centimeters. Try to imagine the resulting litigation!

Initial Syntax Errors

When you run the first compile, you will likely receive a number of syntax errors. In fact, you may receive a relatively large number of syntax errors. Let's return to our earlier source code. As a second illustration of the compile process, suppose we have corrected some of the syntax errors in the code and press the **Compile** button; we see the screen shown in Figure 3.8.

Figure 3.8

Syntax Error Messages

```
--------------------Configuration: myFirstCpp - Win32 Debug--------------------
Compiling...
myFirstCpp.cpp
C:\cppFun\myFirstCpp.cpp(25) : error C2146: syntax error : missing ';' before identifier 'cin'
C:\cppFun\myFirstCpp.cpp(93) : error C2065: 'main' : undeclared identifier
C:\cppFun\myFirstCpp.cpp(104) : fatal error C1004: unexpected end of file found
Error executing cl.exe.

myFirstCpp.obj - 3 error(s), 0 warning(s)
```

In the Debug window (see Figure 3.8), we now see three error messages. The compile failed due to syntax errors in the source code. The programmer will now have to debug the code.

The Art of Debugging

Debugging is an art form and some programmers are better at it than others. All programmers, regardless of their level of experience, must practice debugging. Through practice, programmers become good at solving these problems.

First, it is helpful to begin to develop a plan for debugging the source code. This can save you a great of deal of time and allows you to proceed in a logical fashion. Beginning programmers need all the help they can get on the problems they encounter. A set of steps, like the one outlined here, could help you in your problem solving endeavors. Your instructor may suggest alternative procedures.

Eight steps to debug a problem:

1. Proofread before compiling.
2. Compile.
3. Correct the obvious errors in a single pass.
4. Recompile.
5. Repeat steps 3 and 4 until no further errors are obvious.
6. Attempt to solve the remaining errors in a top-down fashion.
7. Solve whatever errors you can without spending long periods on any given error.
8. Recompile whenever you feel you don't see any further solutions.

Step 1:   Proofread before compiling.

The worst experience for students is to run that first compile when you feel happy about what you have accomplished and have 100–1000 errors occur. It makes the task ahead of you seem insurmountable. Scan your code once before you compile and fix anything you see. You certainly shouldn't try to find every single error because the compiler is a helpful tool to point out errors, but you should try to fix what you can see easily before you press that button.

Step 2:   Compile.

This is the first compile and should result in quite a few errors unless you did a lot of upfront planning and proofing.

Step 3:   Correct the obvious errors in a single pass.

Once you have run that first compile and have obtained a significant number of errors, you have to proceed according to plan. A single syntax error may cause the compiler to believe numerous other syntax errors are occurring. For instance, let's say you mistyped **ofo** when you defined the identifier, **foo** in your program. If you then use **foo** 1500 times in the source code, you will have at least 1500 errors in your program. Thus, you could correct the single error and remove 1500 syntax errors just by correcting one small item.

Look at the error lines and if you see the error, fix it. Otherwise leave it for later. It may vanish when you correct something else.

Scan all the errors, and fix anything immediately obvious, but don't worry too much at this point about things you don't recognize.

One handy feature in Visual C++ is the ability to jump from the error message to the line on which the compiler believes the error occurred. Double-clicking the error message moves the cursor to the line where the compiler detected the error. This is the way to locate all the possible error lines in the code quickly . Remember though, just because an error message has occurred on a given line does not mean there is actually an error on that line. If the error is not obvious to you, leave it, and go to the next error in the list.

Step 4:   Recompile.

Now, you should recompile the source code with the corrections. Hopefully, you will have fewer errors, but don't be alarmed if you suddenly have a lot more. Some syntax errors can mask other errors or even cause the compilation to stop. This is nothing to be alarmed about, just part of the process.

Step 5:   Repeat until no further errors are obvious.

Repeat the first two steps and fix all the obvious errors until you can't find any more obvious solutions. This may take many repeats or it may only take a few, depending on the errors and your level of expertise.

Step 6:   Attempt to solve the remaining errors in top-down fashion.

Now, the hard part, fixing errors when you don't see the immediate problem. In this case one of two things is probably to blame: (1) an error you don't recognize; or (2) an error you might recognize is causing a problem you wouldn't expect it to cause, and the compiler is not smart enough to understand.

The newer you are to programming, the more errors you will never have seen and thus, the more situations will occur in which you don't know the immediate answer. As you practice, you will get used to certain types of errors and they will suggest simple fixes, but you will see puzzling occurrences no matter how long you have been programming. Thus, you need a strategy for solving problems.

Work from the beginning of the program, because in most compilers, the errors are detected from the beginning, sequentially, until the end. Some errors are so severe the compiler will simply refuse to continue.

First, assume your syntax is wrong and verify that you have input the keyword or other elements in the appropriate manner. For C++ syntax, look up the command in a reference book like Gaddis, even if you think it's right and make sure. This will help you learn the syntax and you can verify that your instructions are correct.

You should also add comments, called working comments, to the corrections. This will help you remember what you have changed and how you have changed it. You can use block comments to do this and you might consider numbering them so that you can refer to the numbers later.

Example 3.1

The Block Comment Checklist

```
cuot << "This is a line of code" << endl;
/************Debug*****************
1. Error is undeclared identifier
2. Checked syntax for literal
3. Checked syntax for screen output
      a. Cuot is misspelled
*/
```

This is a simple example, but if you start listing things, it will really help you to work through the debug process. Obviously, before you turn in your source code, you should remove this type of commenting unless you were unable to remove the error. Then your instructor will be able to see what you tried to solve the problem and may be able to quickly identify what the problem is and provide help.

We need a set of steps to attempt to figure out what the problem may be when it is more complex than just a misspelled word. Following is a set of steps for general debugging. The more uncomfortable you feel about the problem, the more a set of structured steps will help you solve it.

Example 3.2

The General Debugging Checklist

1. *Visually verify the spelling and case of keywords and identifiers.*
2. *Verify syntax with a reference book, not just visually.*
3. *Try to find an example in the reference book that does something similar and compare it to your code.*
4. *Verify that the necessary delimiters used for that line are there.*
5. *Without looking at your source code or notes, rewrite the instruction on a piece of paper and then compare it to your source code (don't cheat).*
6. *Verify that the line is really the source of the error by commenting the line out using //.*

   Be advised many other errors may result from doing this, but just worry about the current line and current error for now.

Real World

Structured steps to solving problems will always help. Consider airline pilots. Their jobs are critical, and a tiny mistake can result in catastrophe. Pilots always use checklists for everything. Next time you are getting on a plane and the cabin door is open, notice that pilots have checklists on their laps as they preflight the plane. Even in small single engine planes, pilots use checklists and you will typically find they have a checklist for all the normal procedures and all the possible emergencies. This helps them to make sure they checked everything and that they use logic, even when they are in an emergency. Programmers get frustrated and tired. They spend long hours trying to solve complex problems. Use a checklist to debug programs and you won't forget something. Programming makes us all feel stupid from time to time, but don't forget to follow logical steps and you will spend more time smiling.

Step 1: Visually verify the spelling and case of keywords and identifiers.

This is a common cause of problems and you should quickly review the spelling of keywords. Make sure they appear in blue. If you keywords appear in blue, they are being considered keywords by the compiler. Likewise, make sure your literals and identifiers are not blue or green (indicating they are comments). You should also make sure your identifiers are spelled correctly. As suggested earlier, write down the line of code on paper and then compare all the identifiers back to where they are defined. This technique is particularly helpful if you are having problems with spelling and can't seem to spot the errors. Many beginning programmers have great difficulty spotting spelling errors, particularly in non-standard usage where the words and phrases they are typing are unfamiliar.

Step 2: Verify syntax with a reference book, not just visually.

You should always make sure the syntax is correct, even if your eyes tell you that it is. It is often the case that you glance at something and assume that it is correct and, therefore, miss the problem. As with the spelling problem, you should write the phrase down on a piece of paper and then compare it to a reference book. This forces you to think about the problem and to review it carefully.

Step 3: Try to find an example in the reference book that does something similar and compare it to your code.

Many programmers love to work by example and the more expertise you have, the more you will be able to use this tactic. Find an example and then see if you can figure out where your code differs from the example. If a lot of the code is similar, it may point you to the exact location of the error. Certainly, there are occasions where this does not work, or you simply cannot find an example, but if you can find something similar that works, then you have a window into the problem.

Step 4: Verify that the necessary delimiters used for that line are there.

Delimiters can certainly cause problems. You may want to verify the delimiters on the line above and below the error line as this can sometimes cause errors. Visual C++ has proved reliable at detecting missing delimiters, but as you will see in some later examples, you will find a missing delimiter can cause a very confusing error earlier and/or later in the program. Typically, the errors occur after the missing delimiter.

Step 5: Without looking at your source code or notes, rewrite the instruction on a piece of paper and then compare it to your source code.

This approach helps you to try a second time to write the instruction. You may do something dramatically different in the second version that will tip you off to the error. Students write lines of code when they are distracted or thinking of some other approach, and when they rewrite it later, they use a different approach that helps them solve the error. The critical message here is to not look at the original, problematic source code. If you do that, you will likely just copy down what you already have, and this becomes a pointless exercise.

Step 6: Verify that the line is really the source of the error by commenting the line out with //.

This is a common technique programmers use to work with code in the debugging process. The programmer comments the line out where the error is occurring and then recompiles the code to see what happens. A variety of results may occur and you shouldn't be alarmed if your program suddenly jumps from five errors to 500. Many errors may be caused by the omission of a declaration or other important statements in your source code. Don't worry though; this simply gives you a chance to work with the line in question.

One possible outcome is that the error simply disappears. This is a nice result, since it implies that the error is being caused by the line you are examining. This tells you that you may want to fall back on some of the previous techniques again until you spot exactly what the error is.

A second outcome is that the error moves to the next line. This would imply that the error might be caused by an earlier line of code. In particular, these types of clues often point to missing delimiters preceding the line on which you are working. Remember, that the compiler is not very smart. Don't take its recommendation at face value.

The most important thing the beginning programmer needs to remember is that it will take a great deal of time to resolve all the syntax errors you will make. The second most important lesson is that the compiler cannot be trusted to point you in the right direction. On the simplest of errors, the compiler will always be correct, but as errors become more convoluted, the compiler may make many mistakes with its limited intelligence. Don't be afraid to experiment with comments and other changes to the code to see what happens. Debugging is largely detective work. As you develop your own bag of investigative tricks, you will find it becomes easier.

Philosophy

You should adopt the philosophy "Never make a change you cannot explain." Beginning programmers often feel a sense of desperation setting in about three o'clock in the morning on the day a program is due. This may result in trying desperate things, like sticking in semi-colons or curly braces in response to error messages. You **must** understand why you are doing something. If you can't explain why you just added that semi-colon, then don't do it. Consult your reference books to determine why a semi-colon should or should not go in that location. If you fail to follow this philosophy, you will just create larger problems by random actions.

The second part of the philosophy is "Never trust an error message." All too often, beginning programmers get an error message such as:

```
Missing ; on line 701
```

The natural response is to double-click the message, jump to line 701, and insert a delimiter. Student programs often have lines in them like this:

```
AFunCall(x);;;;;;
```

This results from the programmer getting frantic and continuing to get missing ; messages on the line. Never ever start down this path to the dark side of programming. Always make sure you understand why the error message occurred. Do not rely on random actions to correct problems, or you will end up with a large mess instead of a source code.

Using Microsoft Software Developers Kit [SDK] Help

The Visual C++ environment contains a great deal of help for the product and has a complete library of all the syntax (including a lot of syntax you won't need in a beginning course). The sheer volume of syntax may create some confusion, and many students have found the files to be simply overwhelming and resorted to reference books instead. However, sometimes there is an error message so mysterious you must consult the help sections about it. When you have messages in the error window, it is easy to acquire help on the topic by pressing the **F1** key after single left-clicking on the error message. This will bring up the SDK listing for that particular error. It is also true that error messages leave a lot to be desired in terms of helping you solve the error.

Simple Debugging Tutorial

In an effort to provide you with some practice debugging Visual C++ syntax, a sample program is included here to get you started. You may wish to work through this tutorial after you have started working on your first assignment in Visual C++.

Step 1: Create a subdirectory.

Create a subdirectory on your hard drive, floppy disk, or Zip disk in which to store the file. Name this subdirectory **Tutorial**. Complete the steps as outlined in the following pages.

1. Open the Microsoft Explorer using the **Windows** key and **e**. You should see something like Figure 3.9.

2. Click on the drive on which you wish to create the tutorial. If you choose the C: drive, you should see something like Figure 3.10.

3. Open the **File** menu and choose **New** and **Folder**. You should then see something like Figure 3.11.

Figure 3.9

Creating a Subdirectory for the Tutorial

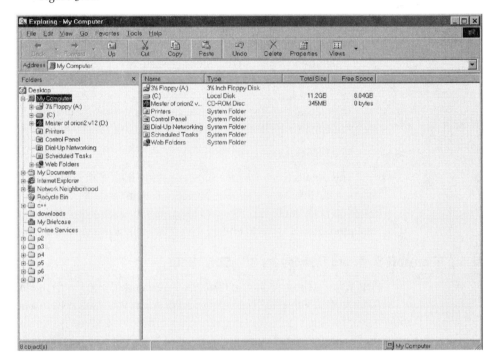

Figure 3.10

The C: Drive

Figure 3.11

The New Folder

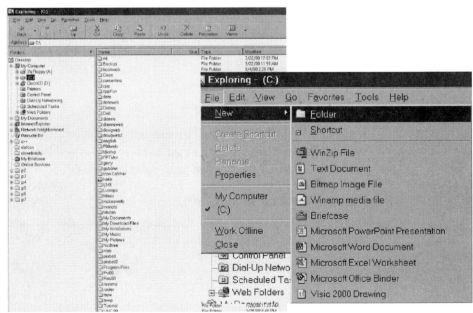

4.	The new folder should appear at the bottom of the screen and be named **NewFolder**, as shown in Figure 3.12.

5.	Rename the new folder by typing **Tutorial** (this assumes there is no other folder on your disk named **Tutorial**). This is shown in Figure 3.13.

6.	Now retrieve the file **debug1.cpp** from the CD that accompanies this book, and save it into the folder you just created. You should see something like Figure 3.14 on page 60.

Figure 3.12

The New Folder Exists

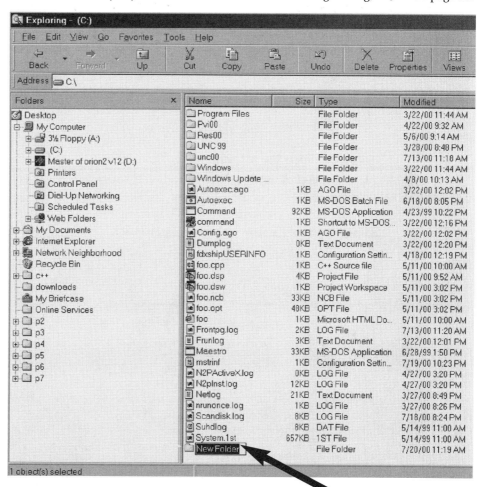

Figure 3.13

Rename the Folder

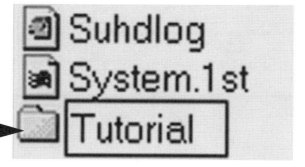

Figure 3.14

The Saved File

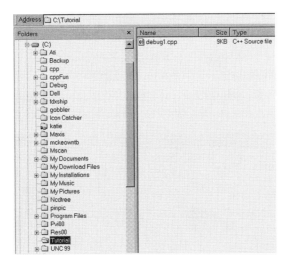

Step 2: Open the program file in Visual C++.

1.   Double-click the file, which should open Visual C++. You should now see something like Figure 3.15.

If you have problems with the file opening, first start Visual C++ and then use **File, Open** to get the file. This is shown in Figure 3.16.

Figure 3.15

Visual C++ and the Tutorial File

```
#include <iostream.h>
#include <cctype>

/*  This program is C++ code to play the game of naughts and crosses.  It is the response
    to a programming assignment for fall 1999 in BACS 286.  This version of the program
    includes the extra credit AI routines to 'learn' to play the game against the user.
    The AI uses a rewards and punishment schema to 'learn'.
*/

//Global Vars
int xScore      = 0
int oScore      = 0;
int whoTurn     = 0;
int moveHolder  = 0;

// function prototypes

void drawGame(char[3][3];            //draws the current board
void clrScreen();                    //simple loop to clear the screen
void clrBoard(char[3][3]);           //clears the board
void showScore();                    //display the score
void pauseIt();                      //hold the screen
void getMove(char[3][3]);            //get a move from a player.
int  badMove(char[3][3], int, int);  //check for an illegal move
int  chkWin(char[3][3]);             //determine if a win exists
void convertMove(int &, int &);      //converts moves to coordinates
void winHandler(char);

//main program begins

void main ()

{
    char    theboard[3][3] = {{' ',' ',' '},{' ',' ',' '},{' ',' ',' '}};
    int     row;                //var for array sub1
    int     col;                //var for array sub2
    char    resp;               //user response var for ys and ns
    int     flag     = 0;       //used to test a first time instruction option
    char    loopResp ='Y';      //controls the game loop
    char    dummy;              //pauses the screen
    Int     movCount = 0;       //to detect a tie
```

Figure 3.16

Alternative
Method to
Open the Tutorial
File

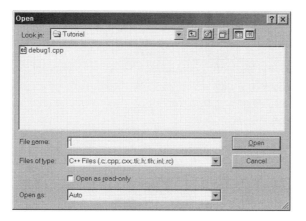

Either method should result in Figure 3.15 appearing on your screen.

Step 3: Run an initial compile.

Now, you need to begin your first debugging session with Visual C++. This tutorial contains a number of simple syntax errors to help you get a feel for what is going on in the debugging process so that you can begin to develop your skill using the steps outlined previously.

1.   Press the **Compile** button to run your first scan of the program. The **Compile** button is shown in Figure 3.17.

2.   You will see the compile run, and two errors should appear in the lower window. They are shown in Figure 3.18. (You may have to acknowledge the creation of a default workspace for the program. Select **Yes** to create this workspace so the compiler has a folder in which to store all the files.)

Figure 3.17

The Compile
Button

Figure 3.18

The First Two
Errors

3. Now, double-click on the first error to jump to that line of the program. The error is

c:\tutorial\debug1.cpp(12) : error C2144: syntax error : missing ';' before type 'int'

which indicates that there is a missing semi-colon (delimiter) somewhere on that line. In this case, the compiler actually tells you that the missing delimiter is before the keyword **int**. This means, that the error is not actually on the line but before it. This is shown in Figure 3.19.

As you practice debugging, errors like this will become very easy to spot and repair.

Figure 3.19

The Missing Delimiter

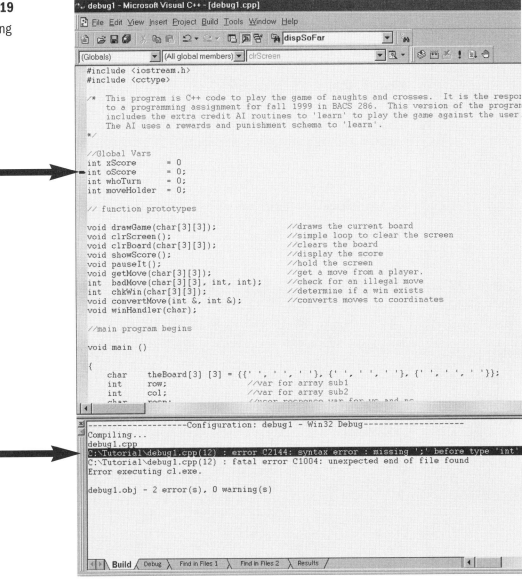

4. Correct the error by adding the semi-colon on the line:

   ```
   int xScore    = 0;
   ```

5. Save the source code by pressing **File, Save**.

6. Recompile the source code by pressing the **Compile** button again.

7. Uh oh, now, you have a more errors instead of fewer (14 to be exact). This is shown in Figure 3.20.

   In the earlier compile, some error caused the compile to stop. Sometimes the compiler simply cannot deal with errors and is forced to discontinue compiling at that point. That has happened here. The good news is that several of these error messages may be caused by a single error. This is why we want to work from the top down in the program.

Figure 3.20

More Errors

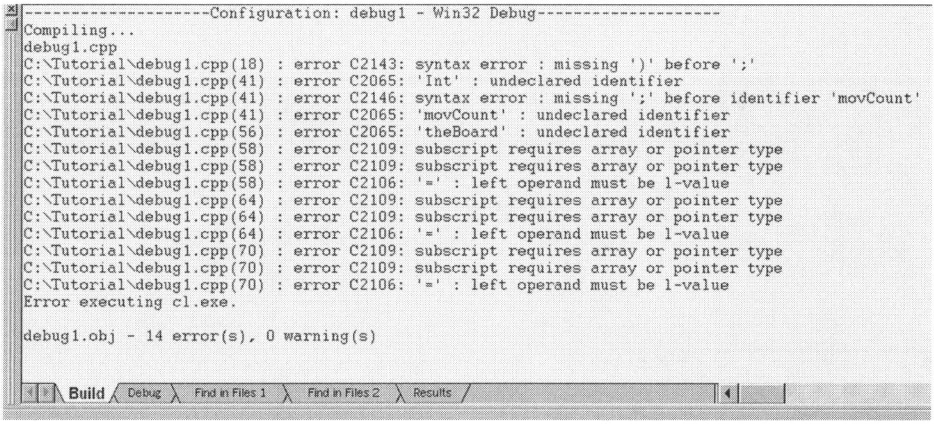

Figure 3.21

The Missing)
Error

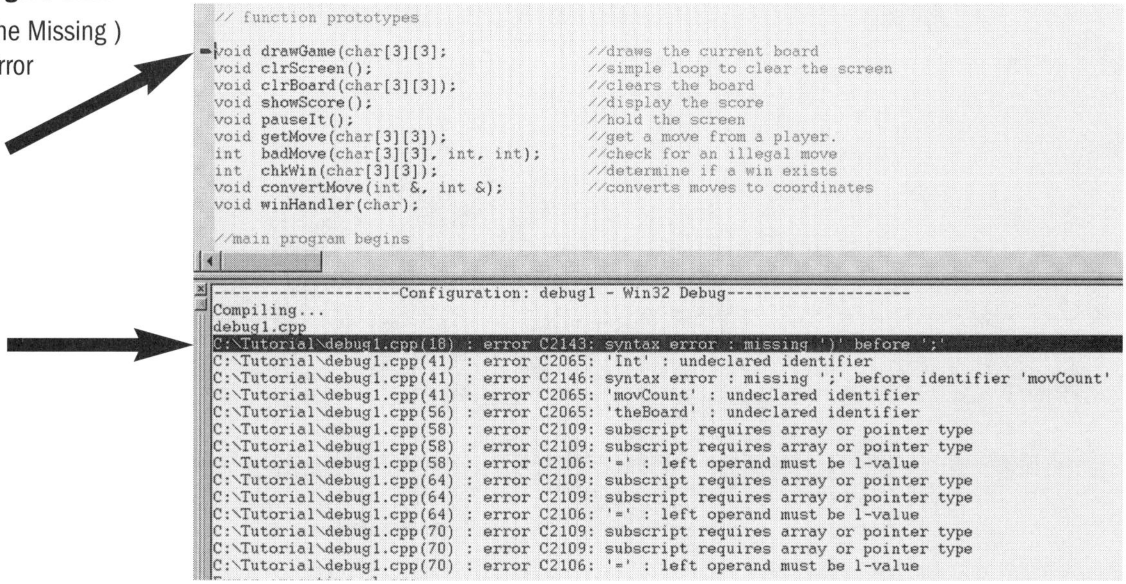

8. Double-click the first error and let's see where it is, as shown in Figure 3.21 on the previous page (63).

```
C:\Tutorial\debug1.cpp(18) : error C2143: syntax error : missing ')' before ';'
```

The message implies there is a missing close parenthesis on this line somewhere. You should always remember that if you open a parenthesis, you have to close it. If you look carefully at the line, you will see there is no closing parenthesis on it. You may also have no idea where the parenthesis should go if you are unfamiliar with the syntax. If you are unsure, the worst thing you can do is to just start adding in parentheses trying to get rid of the error. The message does imply the parenthesis should appear before the delimiter, so let's assume you look up the syntax for this statement and realize the parenthesis should appear between the square bracket (]) and the semi-colon (;).

9. Add the parenthesis, save, and recompile with the **Compile** button. The result is shown in Figure 3.22.

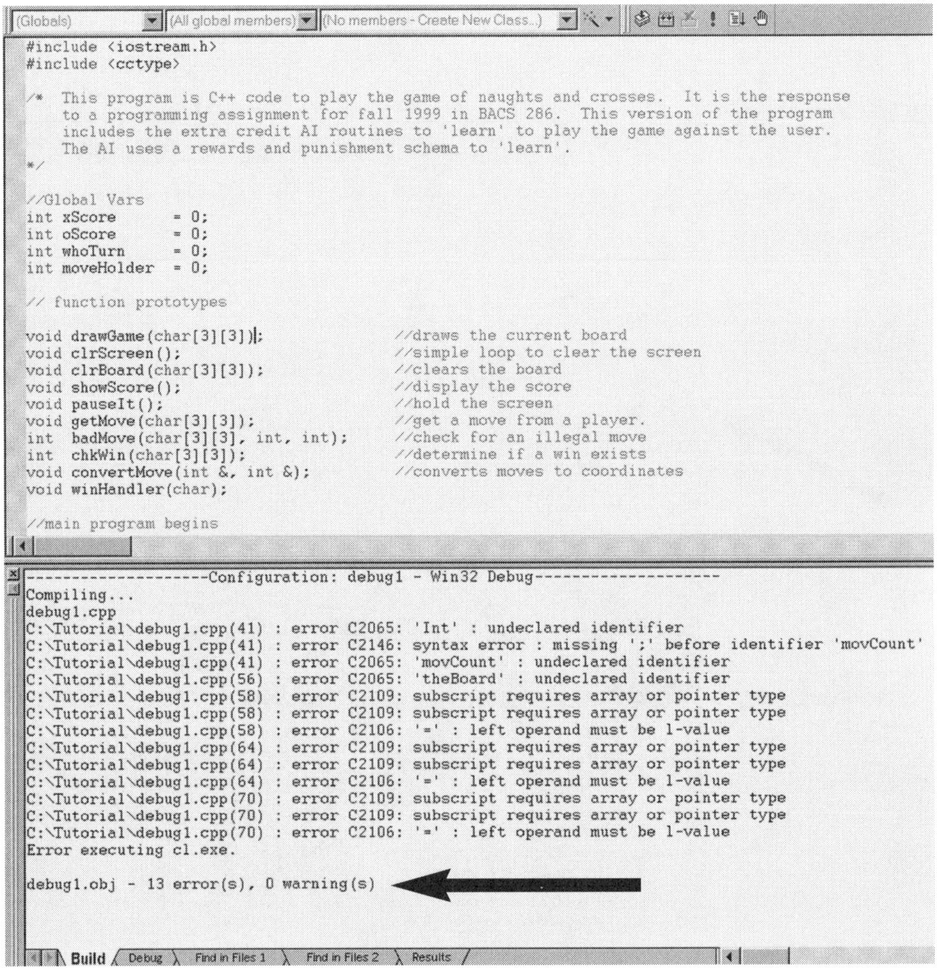

Figure 3.22

13 Errors Left

10. Let's look at the next error, double-click to jump to the line:

```
C:\Tutorial\debug1.cpp(41) : error C2065: 'Int' : undeclared identifier
```

This is an undeclared identifier error. These are very common errors that all program-mers deal with every time they write programs. The error usually means a misspelled word, a typo, or something similar. These errors can often cause many additional errors because if the identifier is not defined, every one of its occurrences in the program will result in an error message. Again, you need to look closely at the line to see what is wrong. The message says Int is undeclared and we will assume you know that Int is supposed to be a keyword so it should be blue, but it's not! Look up the syntax for the **int** keyword in a reference book. You realize that **int** cannot have a capital I in front of it or it's not a keyword. This is an important lesson to remember for C++: the case of everything matters. Case errors may be as simple as an identifier x not being equal to X in C++. In typing class, we were trained to start each sentence with a capital letter. Thus, case errors are often difficult for beginning programmers to avoid and to spot.

11. Correct the Int error by changing I to **i**, save, and recompile. The result is shown in Figure 3.23.

Figure 3.23

The Corrected Int Error

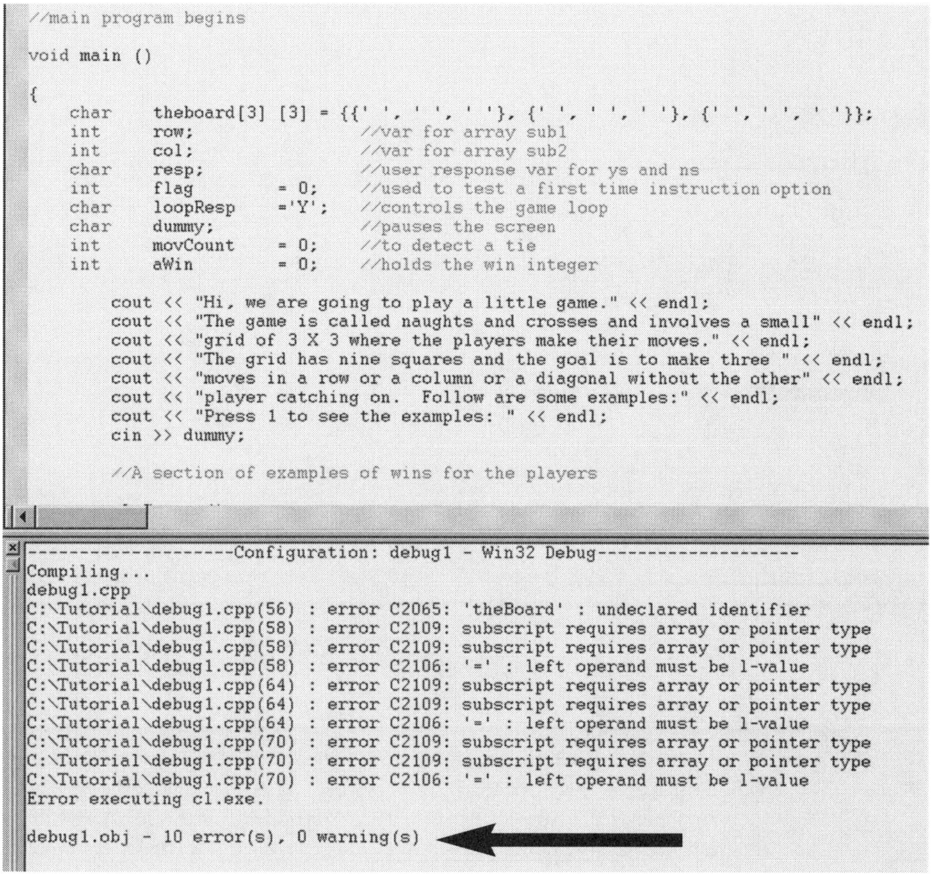

```
//main program begins

void main ()

{
    char    theboard[3] [3] = {{' ',' ',' '}, {' ',' ',' '}, {' ',' ',' '}};
    int     row;                //var for array sub1
    int     col;                //var for array sub2
    char    resp;               //user response var for ys and ns
    int     flag      = 0;      //used to test a first time instruction option
    char    loopResp  ='Y';     //controls the game loop
    char    dummy;              //pauses the screen
    int     movCount  = 0;      //to detect a tie
    int     aWin      = 0;      //holds the win integer

        cout << "Hi, we are going to play a little game." << endl;
        cout << "The game is called naughts and crosses and involves a small" << endl;
        cout << "grid of 3 X 3 where the players make their moves." << endl;
        cout << "The grid has nine squares and the goal is to make three " << endl;
        cout << "moves in a row or a column or a diagonal without the other" << endl;
        cout << "player catching on.  Follow are some examples:" << endl;
        cout << "Press 1 to see the examples: " << endl;
        cin >> dummy;

        //A section of examples of wins for the players
```

```
--------------------Configuration: debug1 - Win32 Debug--------------------
Compiling...
debug1.cpp
C:\Tutorial\debug1.cpp(56) : error C2065: 'theBoard' : undeclared identifier
C:\Tutorial\debug1.cpp(58) : error C2109: subscript requires array or pointer type
C:\Tutorial\debug1.cpp(58) : error C2109: subscript requires array or pointer type
C:\Tutorial\debug1.cpp(58) : error C2106: '=' : left operand must be l-value
C:\Tutorial\debug1.cpp(64) : error C2109: subscript requires array or pointer type
C:\Tutorial\debug1.cpp(64) : error C2109: subscript requires array or pointer type
C:\Tutorial\debug1.cpp(64) : error C2106: '=' : left operand must be l-value
C:\Tutorial\debug1.cpp(70) : error C2109: subscript requires array or pointer type
C:\Tutorial\debug1.cpp(70) : error C2109: subscript requires array or pointer type
C:\Tutorial\debug1.cpp(70) : error C2106: '=' : left operand must be l-value
Error executing cl.exe.

debug1.obj - 10 error(s), 0 warning(s)
```

Well, that got rid of some more errors and left us with only 10. You see that some of the later errors were echoes of the case error. This is another argument in favor of the top-down approach.

12. Double-click on the next error and look at the line:

```
C:\Tutorial\debug1.cpp(56) : error C2065: 'theBoard' : undeclared identifier
```

Now, you should see Figure 3.24:

This is a function call, which may be unfamiliar to you. Again, you may look up the syntax for a function call, and if you do, you will find that the format is correct. The message indicates that theBoard is undeclared. You may or may not be aware that this is not a declaration, but merely a usage of the name (identifier) theBoard. Thus, the error must be in either the declaration or in the local usage on this line. The most common reason for this type of error is misspelled names or the misuse of case. Look back to the declaration of theBoard as shown in Figure 3.25.

You should see that the declaration is theboard not theBoard. Here, you have to make a judgment call about which is incorrect, the declaration or the use on line 51. If you wrote the source code, you should know what conventions you have used for naming identifiers, but you may sometimes be looking at someone else's source code. Quickly scan the program and see if there are other occurrences of theboard or theBoard.[*] This is shown in Figure 3.26.

Figure 3.24

Line 51 Error

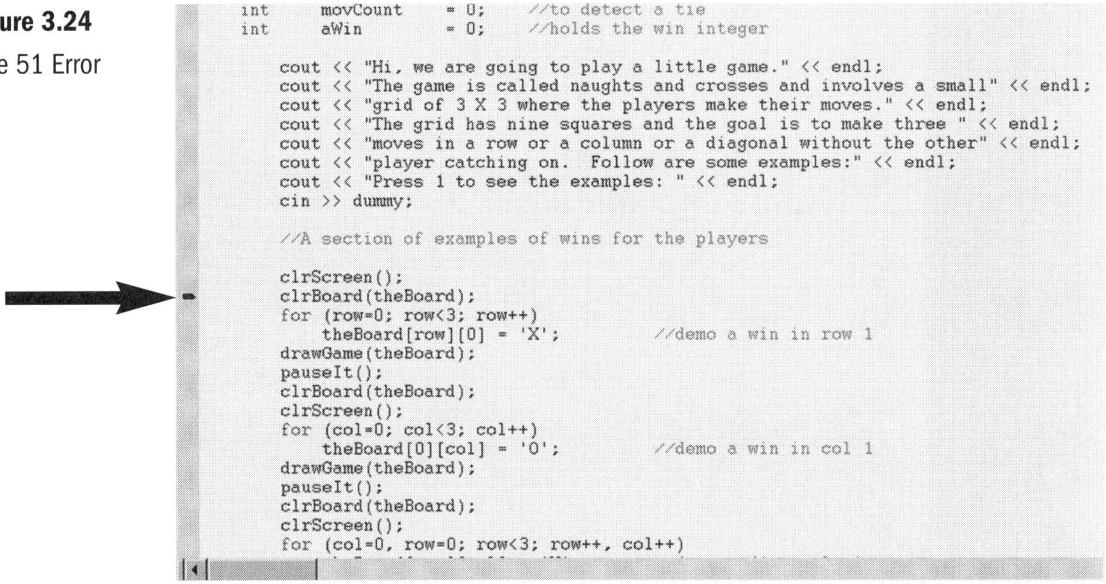

```
int     movCount   = 0;    //to detect a tie
int     aWin       = 0;    //holds the win integer

   cout << "Hi, we are going to play a little game." << endl;
   cout << "The game is called naughts and crosses and involves a small" << endl;
   cout << "grid of 3 X 3 where the players make their moves." << endl;
   cout << "The grid has nine squares and the goal is to make three " << endl;
   cout << "moves in a row or a column or a diagonal without the other" << endl;
   cout << "player catching on.  Follow are some examples:" << endl;
   cout << "Press 1 to see the examples: " << endl;
   cin >> dummy;

   //A section of examples of wins for the players

   clrScreen();
   clrBoard(theBoard);
   for (row=0; row<3; row++)
       theBoard[row][0] = 'X';        //demo a win in row 1
   drawGame(theBoard);
   pauseIt();
   clrBoard(theBoard);
   clrScreen();
   for (col=0; col<3; col++)
       theBoard[0][col] = 'O';        //demo a win in col 1
   drawGame(theBoard);
   pauseIt();
   clrBoard(theBoard);
   clrScreen();
   for (col=0, row=0; row<3; row++, col++)
```

---

[*] Note that C++ will allow the use of both theboard and theBoard, as well as any other variant, considering them different identifiers. This is a poor practice and serves to confuse the programmer, the analyst, and anyone else trying to review the source code. Nevertheless, you should be aware that it may be done and take care to avoid multiple declarations. In this program, you will not find a second declaration.

Figure 3.25

theBoard
Declaration

```
void winHandler(char);

//main program begins

void main ()

{
    char    theboard[3] [3] = {{' ',' ',' '}, {' ',' ',' '}, {' ',' ',' '}};
    int     row;                //var for array sub1
    int     col;                //var for array sub2
    char    resp;               //user response var for ys and ns
    int     flag      = 0;      //used to test a first time instruction option
    char    loopResp  ='Y';     //controls the game loop
    char    dummy;              //pauses the screen
    int     movCount  = 0;      //to detect a tie
    int     aWin      = 0;      //holds the win integer

        cout << "Hi, we are going to play a little game." << endl;
        cout << "The game is called naughts and crosses and involves a small" << endl;
        cout << "grid of 3 X 3 where the players make their moves." << endl;
        cout << "The grid has nine squares and the goal is to make three " << endl;
        cout << "moves in a row or a column or a diagonal without the other" << endl;
        cout << "player catching on.  Follow are some examples:" << endl;
        cout << "Press 1 to see the examples: " << endl;
        cin >> dummy;

        //A section of examples of wins for the players

        clrScreen();
```

Figure 3.26

theBoard
Observation

```
        cout << "grid of 3 X 3 where the players make their moves." << endl;
        cout << "The grid has nine squares and the goal is to make three " << endl;
        cout << "moves in a row or a column or a diagonal without the other" << endl;
        cout << "player catching on.  Follow are some examples:" << endl;
        cout << "Press 1 to see the examples: " << endl;
        cin >> dummy;

        //A section of examples of wins for the players

        clrScreen();
        clrBoard(theBoard);
        for (row=0; row<3; row++)
            theBoard[row][0] = 'X';         //demo a win in row 1
        drawGame(theBoard);
        pauseIt();
        clrBoard(theBoard);
        clrScreen();
        for (col=0; col<3; col++)
            theBoard[0][col] = 'O';         //demo a win in col 1
        drawGame(theBoard);
        pauseIt();
        clrBoard(theBoard);
        clrScreen();
        for (col=0, row=0; row<3; row++, col++)
            theBoard[row][col] = 'X';       //demo a diagonal win
        drawGame(theBoard);
        pauseIt();
        clrBoard(theBoard);
        clrScreen();
```

You immediately see repeated usage of the theBoard and no other usage of theboard. This implies that theBoard is likely the correct declaration.

13. Change the declaration line from theboard to **theBoard**, save, and recompile. The result is shown in Figure 3.27 on the following page (68).

Wow! All of the errors are gone. This is a classic example of a single error resulting in many additional problems. This concludes the tutorial on basic syntax debugging. You should remember to follow the steps outlined earlier when you attempt this with your own program.

Figure 3.27

Errors Resolved

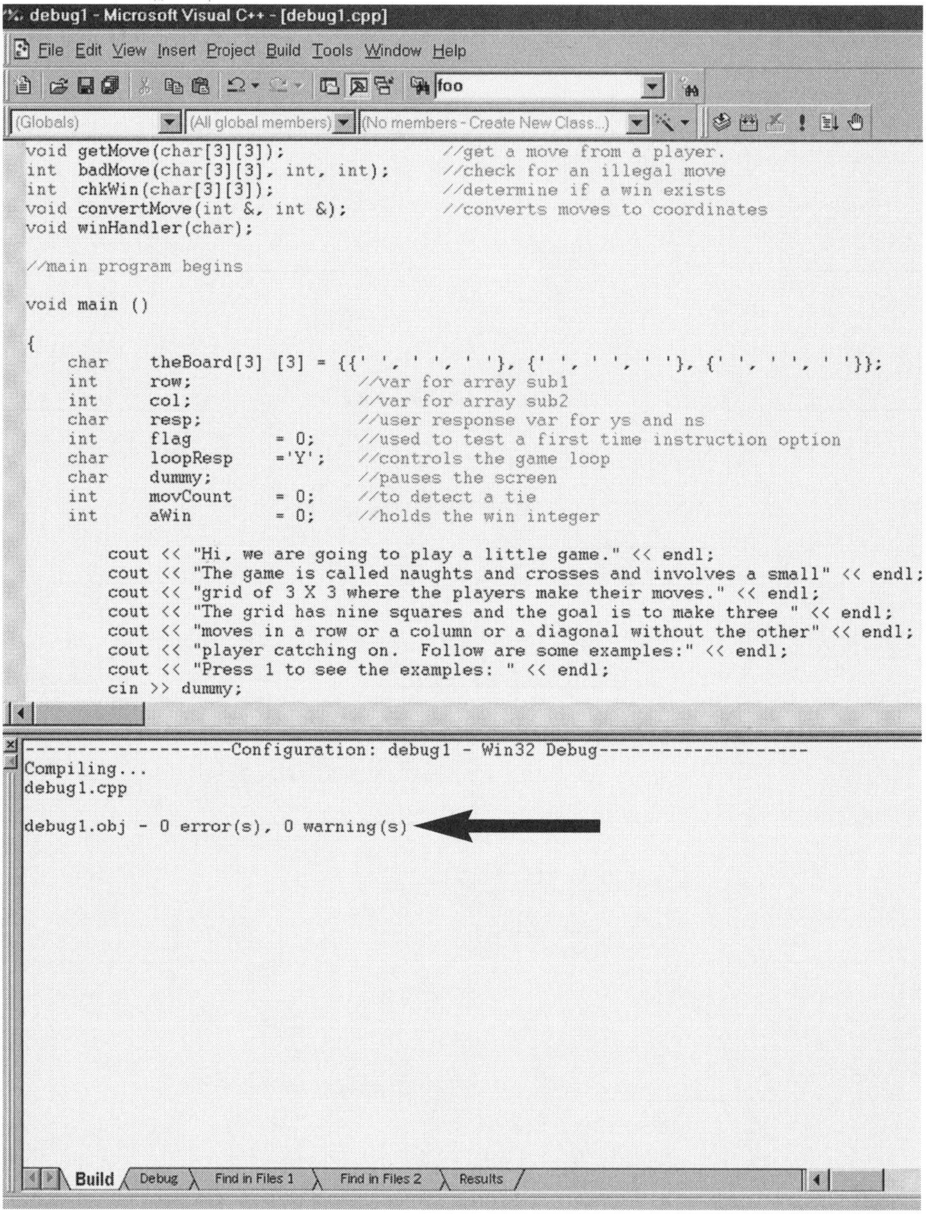

```
debug1 - Microsoft Visual C++ - [debug1.cpp]
 File Edit View Insert Project Build Tools Window Help

                                              foo

(Globals)          (All global members)   (No members - Create New Class...)

void getMove(char[3][3]);               //get a move from a player.
int  badMove(char[3][3], int, int);     //check for an illegal move
int  chkWin(char[3][3]);                //determine if a win exists
void convertMove(int &, int &);         //converts moves to coordinates
void winHandler(char);

//main program begins

void main ()

{
    char     theBoard[3] [3] = {{' ', ' ', ' '}, {' ', ' ', ' '}, {' ', ' ', ' '}};
    int      row;                  //var for array sub1
    int      col;                  //var for array sub2
    char     resp;                 //user response var for ys and ns
    int      flag      = 0;        //used to test a first time instruction option
    char     loopResp  ='Y';       //controls the game loop
    char     dummy;                //pauses the screen
    int      movCount  = 0;        //to detect a tie
    int      aWin      = 0;        //holds the win integer

        cout << "Hi, we are going to play a little game." << endl;
        cout << "The game is called naughts and crosses and involves a small" << endl;
        cout << "grid of 3 X 3 where the players make their moves." << endl;
        cout << "The grid has nine squares and the goal is to make three " << endl;
        cout << "moves in a row or a column or a diagonal without the other" << endl;
        cout << "player catching on.  Follow are some examples:" << endl;
        cout << "Press 1 to see the examples: " << endl;
        cin >> dummy;

--------------------Configuration: debug1 - Win32 Debug--------------------
Compiling...
debug1.cpp

debug1.obj - 0 error(s), 0 warning(s)  ←

  Build  Debug   Find in Files 1   Find in Files 2   Results
```

Common Syntax Errors

In this section, we present an initial discussion of syntax errors and some possible solutions on the level of beginning programmers. The reader should understand that it is not possible to illustrate every conceivable error, nor is it possible to describe all of the circumstances that generate errors. Instead, the goal is to reveal errors that are very common among first-time programmers and to show how these errors occur and how to resolve them in your programs. The assumption of this section is that you are actually to the point of working on your programs in Visual C++ and have some experience now with syntax. This book does not attempt to describe C++ syntax, and you should refer to your course materials or STARTING OUT WITH C++ by Tony Gaddis for references to C++ syntax and programming.

In each section of the error discussion, I will provide you with a general discussion of the type of error (that could apply to most any language); an example showing the error in Visual C++ and the error number and statement from the Visual C++ compiler. Remember, not all errors are covered, merely common errors that occur with greater frequency for beginning programmers.

The Missing Name (Undeclared Identifier)

One of the errors most commonly encountered by beginning programmers is the misuse of either a keyword or a name the programmer attempted to define (called a variable). This type of error is common to every programming language but may be described differently by different compilers. The Visual C++ compiler describes it as an undeclared identifier error and is usually able to directly point to the line of source code in which this error is detected. This error is shown in Figure 3.28.

Figure 3.28

The Undeclared Identifier

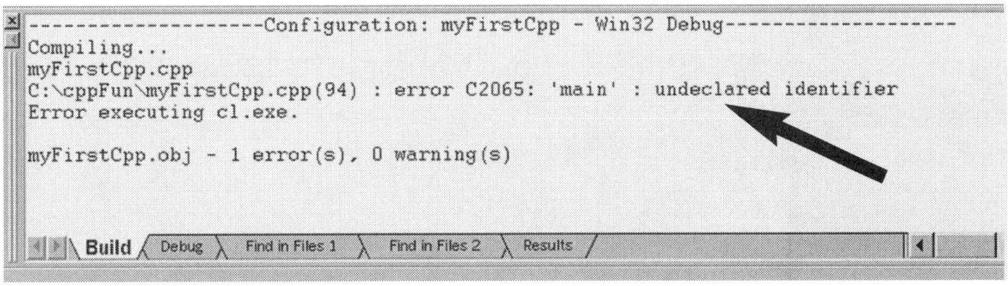

Several things may produce this error:

1. The misspelling of a keyword

2. The misspelling of a programmer defined name (identifier)

3. The misuse of case in a keyword

4. The misuse of case in an identifier

5. The failure to declare an identifier

In each of the circumstances, the compiler thinks that the programmer has used an identifier that has not been declared. For example, suppose you used a keyword, **get**, but instead of using it properly, you input it as **GET**. Now, remember that Visual C++ is case sensitive and everything is based on ASCII numbers such that get ≠ GET ≠Get ≠ gET and so forth. It is very easy when you are typing to misuse case. If the compiler encounters the keyword, GET, it thinks this is some new identifier the programmer was trying to create but has forgotten to define for the compiler. Thus, a syntax error of the undeclared identifier type occurs.

When you encounter an undeclared identifier error in Visual C++ you should first go to the line where the error occurred.

Delimiter Errors

Another common error for all programmers is the misuse/omission of delimiters. Modern programming languages are usually based on delimited phrases instead of the columnar restrictions used in the past. This means that the programmer must tell the compiler where the instruction ends because there is no column/line restriction on the instruction. In Visual C++, the delimiter is the semi-colon (;). Beginning programmers have a lot of difficulty with this because the semi-colon is unfamiliar. Thus, the most common delimiter error is shown:

```
C:\Tutorial\debug1.cpp(27) : error C2146: syntax error : missing ';' before identifier 'winHandler'
```

The C2146 error, which tells you that there is a missing semi-colon, is very common. Most of the time, this error reflects a problem on the preceding line in the form of a missing delimiter. The real danger for the beginning programmer is to fail to understand the error, the error message, and the action to take. Therefore, make sure you really understand why and where to put the delimiter.

A second type of delimiter error involves the use of braces, brackets, and parentheses in Visual C++. These mistakes can result in complicated errors that are difficult to resolve. Such an error is shown in Figure 3.29.

Figure 3.29

A Delimiter Error with Braces

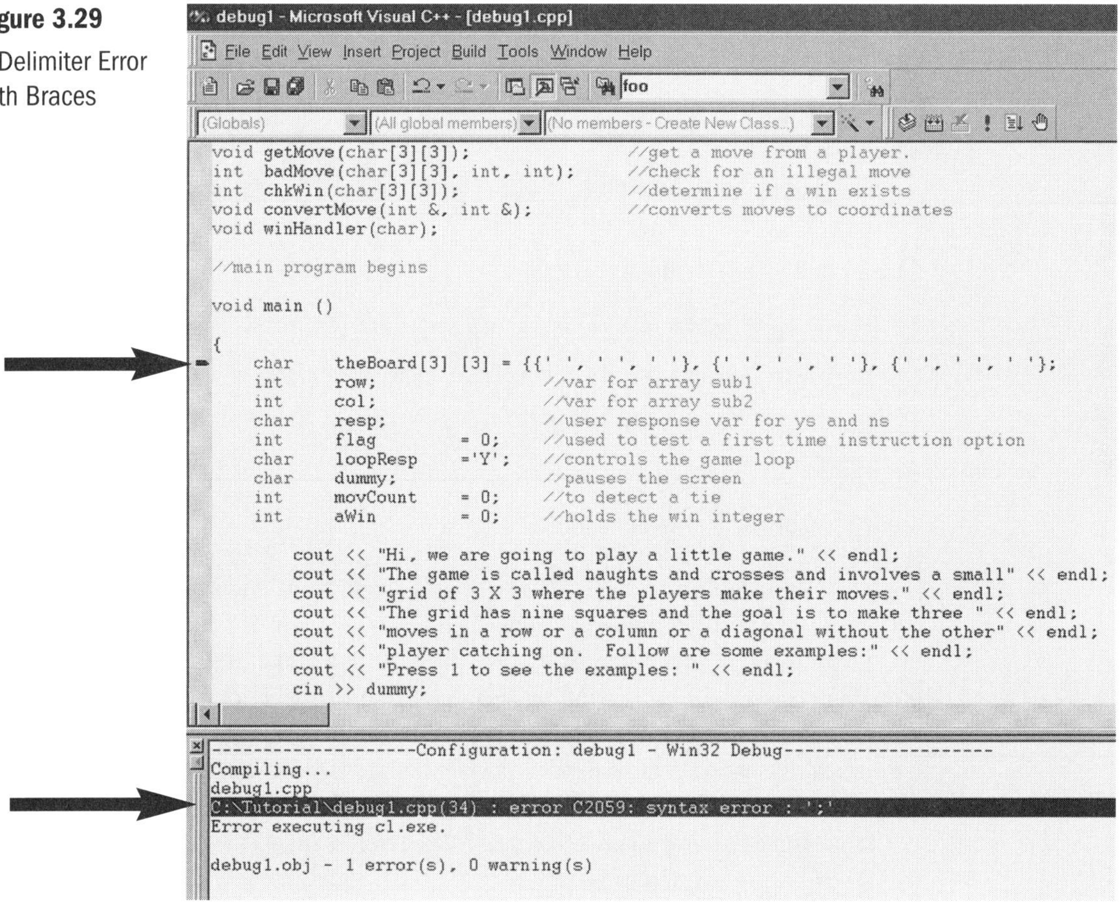

This error seems to imply there is a problem with the semi-colon delimiter on this line. You must be careful here because removal of the delimiter would be disastrous. This is a tricky error even if you are familiar with the syntax, because it is caused by the lack of a closing brace. For a single line, you should always count the opens and then count closes to see if you end up with an equal number. If you have more opens than closes on the line, you have found the problem. In Figure 3.29, it's a missing brace at the end of the line. As a beginning programmer, you may need a lot of time to look up syntax for this type of error. This is another example of the philosophy, "Never trust an error message."

Missing closes can result in other horrible messes, as shown in Figure 3.30.

The poor beginning programmer who gets such a collection of error messages usually ends up in the instructor's office feeling like there is no solution to this problem and then the instructor fixes it in about 10 seconds. The real secret here is knowing what to look for in the error log. It's the last message that you should see:

```
C:\Tutorial\debug1.cpp(416) : fatal error C1004: unexpected end of file found
```

Figure 3.30

A Horrible Mess with Delimiters

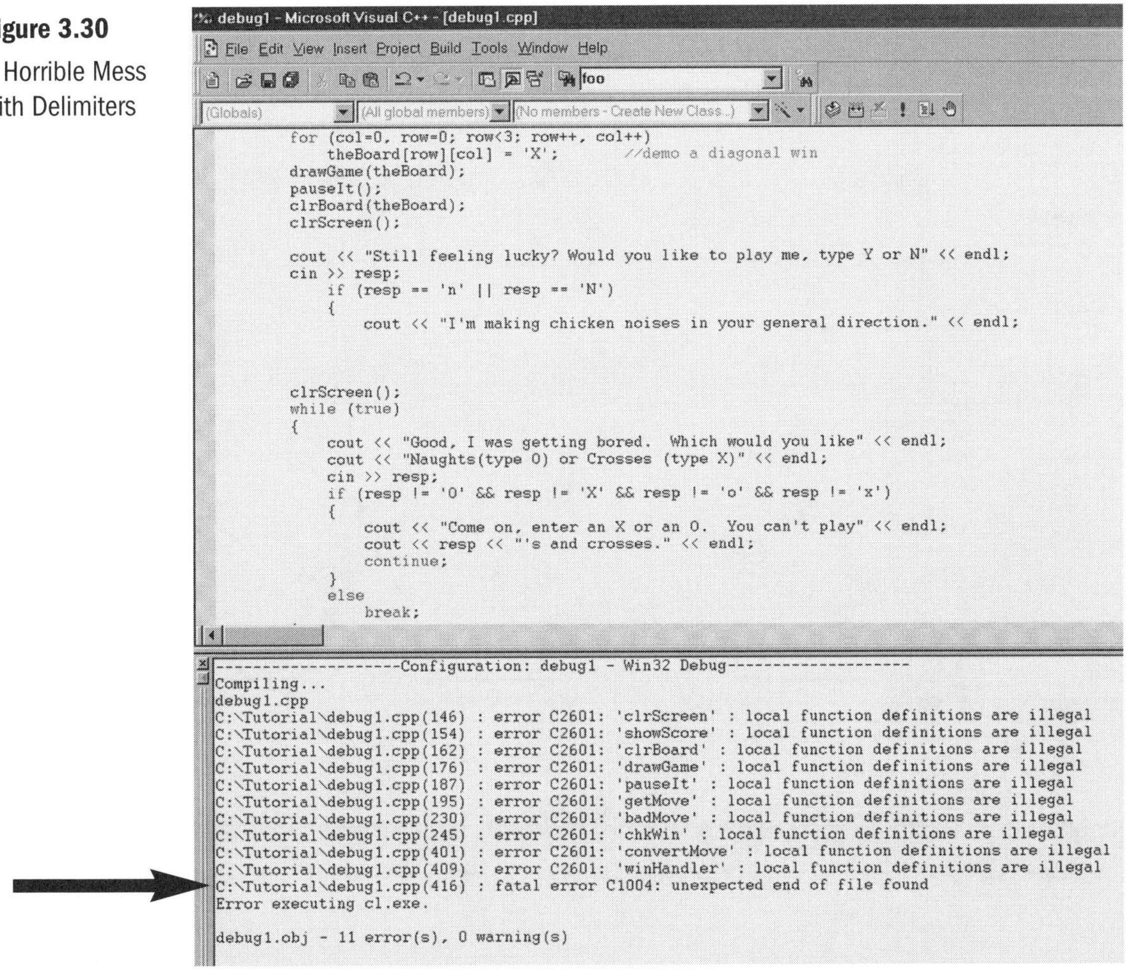

This error message is a huge clue that there is a missing } delimiter or an extra delimiter in your file somewhere. It is likely that many of the other errors are the result of this one. You will have a difficult time flipping through all the pages of code trying to find all the delimiters and match them up. Even experienced programmers have difficulty with this. You need a trick.

Use the outline approach to delimiters. Each time you have an open delimiter, {, put a comment after the delimiter on the line in outline form, // I, // II, etc. For each sublevel of delimiter, use the outline approach, //A, //1, //a, etc. and then do the same thing as they close, so that the last delimiter in the program, }, should match the outline for the first delimiter. If you don't end up back at //I you have omitted a delimiter, and if you are already at //I before you reach the end, you may have some extras.

Warnings

Most any compiler will also provide warnings to the programmer about certain types of actions that may represent problems but do not cause the compiler to flag an error. The inclination of most beginning programmers is to ignore warnings because the program will compile, even with hundreds of warnings. This is a bad habit and can lead to logic errors and other problems later in the compile process. Resolve warnings as well as errors.

Perhaps the most common warning students receive is a typecasting warning. This warning can be seen in Figure 3.31.

Figure 3.31

A Typecasting
Warning

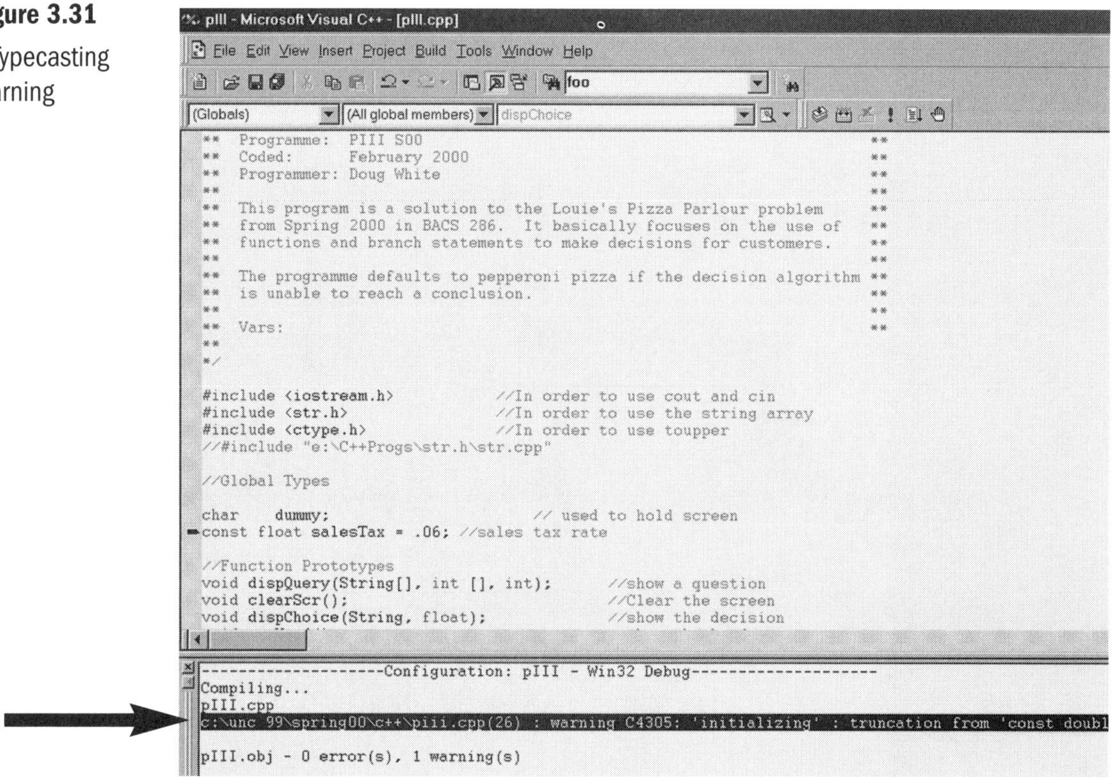

The compiler issues this type of warning whenever one type of number is converted to another type without the inclusion of a typecasting operation. The best example of the need for such a warning would be an attempt to store the value of π in an integer. π (Pi) is approximately equal to 3.14... and if this value were moved to an integer it would be truncated by the compiler to 3. This would cause serious logic errors in any output. Thus, in Figure 3.31, it is necessary to perform what is called a typecast operation to notify the compiler that the programmer fully understands what he or she is doing and wants to do it anyway.

Any time a number is moved from one type to another in Visual C++, a typecasting operation must be performed. (You will learn about other reasons for this operation in your studies of Visual C++.) When you receive a warning similar to Figure 3.31, you need to investigate and decide if you really do want to typecast a number.

In Figure 3.31, the literal number .06 is being moved into a float type identifier in Visual C++. All literals are considered double precision types by default, so when this double type is moved into a float type (which has a smaller storage area) there is the potential to lose data. Anyone can see that .06 is not going to lose any data during the move, so a typecast here is perfectly legitimate. Figure 3.32 illustrates the removal of the warning.

Figure 3.32

The Elimination of a Typecasting Warning

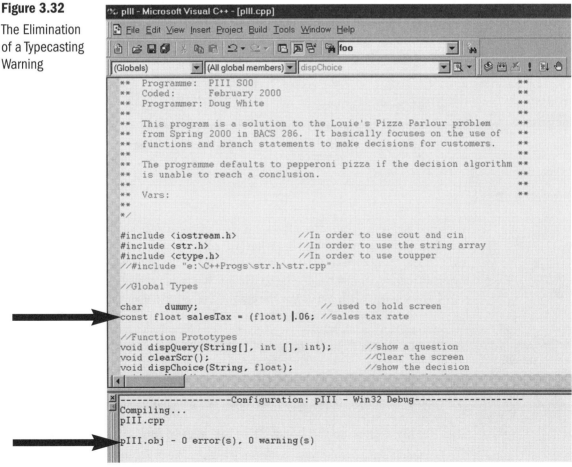

As a programmer, you should remember that you should always understand why something is being done and not just react to a warning or error. Doing so can lead you to serious problems that are difficult to detect.

Your instructor may wish to discuss some of the other types of warnings with you. Never be satisfied with a program that is anything less than one hundred percent.

Disk Space Limitations

A final note about the initial compilation process is the disk space limitation. When using Visual C++, it is not uncommon for students to save their work to floppy disks. The standard 3.5-inch floppy disk has about 1.44 megabytes of disk space available. This is plenty for storage of most introductory level C++ course's source codes. The problems arise because (1) students save too much work to the same floppy and (2) the compiled object and library files, as well as the executable files, can take up considerably more space than the source code alone. If the floppy is full or becomes full during the compilation process, the compile will fail and an error message will be generated. An example is seen in Figure 3.33.

In Figure 3.33, you see the cryptic error messages generated by a failure to compile due to disk space limitations. Many students fail to recognize this problem and spend a lot of time trying to resolve this error. Unfortunately, I cannot tell you how much space is needed for a given source code compile and there are other errors that may occur depending on where in the compile process the overflow happens.

Figure 3.33

Disk Space
Problems

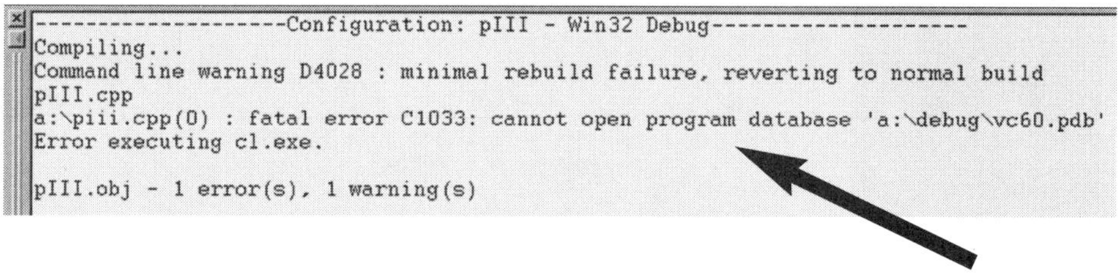

```
-------------------Configuration: pIII - Win32 Debug-------------------
Compiling...
Command line warning D4028 : minimal rebuild failure, reverting to normal build
pIII.cpp
a:\piii.cpp(0) : fatal error C1033: cannot open program database 'a:\debug\vc60.pdb'
Error executing cl.exe.

pIII.obj - 1 error(s), 1 warning(s)
```

Formatting Disks

Many students work in labs where there is no hard drive space available, and no Zip or other removable storage media. When this is the case, a floppy disk may be the only means of storage. Consider using Zip disks for your programs, but if you can't, try using a blank floppy disk for each program. Format the disk before you use it to make sure other work is not already stored. (Remember: when you format the disk, all the material on it will be lost forever.) The following steps will walk you through the formatting process:

Step 1:   Open the Explorer by pressing Windows and e keys simultaneously.

Step 2:   Verify the disk contents before proceeding.

Double-click on the floppy drive. You should see something like Figure 3.34.

Step 3:   Right-click on the floppy drive you wish to format.

You should see a pop-up menu something like the one in Figures 3.34 and 3.35

Figure 3.34

Floppy Drive
Contents

Figure 3.35

Right-Click on the
Floppy Drive

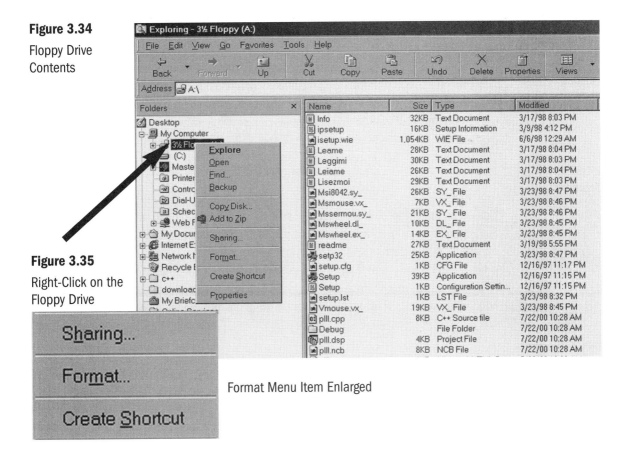

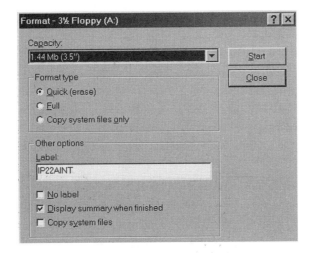

Format Menu Item Enlarged

Figure 3.36

Choose Format

Step 4:   Choose Format on the menu.

Figure 3.36 shows the dialog box that appears when **Format** is chosen.

Step 5:   Click Start.

If this is a new disk, you may only be able to choose **Full** formatting in the dialog box shown in Figure 3.36. Quick formatting, the default, is merely a means to erase all the files on a disk. Full formatting completely rebuilds the disk structure and is actually preferred as it refreshes the disk and verifies there is no problem with the floppy disk.

Remember to make backup copies of your work after saving; you may want to format two floppies while you are at it. Floppy disks are notorious for failing, especially on the days that assignments are due.

Typing Problems

One other common problem worthy of note is the problem with the **L** key in typing. Many typists learned that typing the lowercase **l** was much faster than typing a **1** (one) on the number line above the letter keys. These two symbols have different values and can cause horrendous problems in C++. Be sure to use a 1 (one) when you are doing numerics. **0** (zero) and **O** are also often interchanged, but at least they look different if you study them closely. The **1** (one) and the **l** (ell) look the same, but will cause dramatic differences in your program.

Building Files

With luck and hard work, you will be able to remove all those syntax errors at some point. This leads to a successful compile of the program and the creation of all the files the compiler needs to build an executable (**.exe**) file that you can run. The bad news is that not all syntax errors are detectable by the compiler. There are errors that do not become apparent until the linker attempts to join all the files together in the **.exe**. The good news is that the linker will generate an error message to warn you of such problem. The worst news is that these error messages are usually not associated with any given line in the program.

The example in Figure 3.37 compiles just fine, but an error message is generated when a build is attempted on the program.

This error is confusing and you will find that double-clicking on the error message no longer works at all, because the compiler has approved the source code as complying with the syntax rules of C++. This means you have somehow managed to break the rules without breaking the rules. The best example is to use English as a syntax base. Now, you know a lot of rules and that the words to and two and too are often misused. So, suppose you wrote this sentence:

I want two send to letters too you and you to.

Wow, what a mess. Now, an interesting thing is that most native speakers of English, even your seventh-grade English teacher, could make sense of this sentence despite the misused words. Another interesting thing is that a word processor's spell checker and grammar checker might not indicate any problem with this sentence. Even worse, someone with limited or missing skills in English trying to translate this sentence with a dictionary would likely decide to study ancient Coptic instead of English.

Figure 3.37

A Linker Error

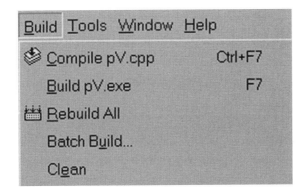

```
PV - Microsoft Visual C++ - [PV.cpp]
File Edit View Insert Project Build Tools Window Help

(Globals)          (All global members)    dispsoFar

void showClues(char clue[])
//display a clue from the parallel array
{
    cout << clue << endl;
}

void blankIt(char buildArray[], int size)
//fill the array with *s
{
    for (int x = 0; x < size ; x++)
    {
        buildArray[x] = '*';
    }
}

void dispsoFar(char buildArray [], int size)
//display the guesses so far
{
    cout << "So far you have:" << endl;
    for (int x = 0; x < size; x++)
    {
        cout << "-" << buildArray[x];
    }
    cout << endl;
}

void aGuess(char known[], char guess[], int &theWins, int &theLosses, bool &aWinner, int size)
//check their phrase guess

------------------Configuration: PV - Win32 Debug------------------
Compiling...
PV.cpp
Linking...
PV.obj : error LNK2001: unresolved external symbol "void __cdecl dispSoFar(char * const,int)" (?dispSoFar@@YAXQADH@Z)
Debug/PV.exe : fatal error LNK1120: 1 unresolved externals
Error executing link.exe.

PV.exe - 2 error(s), 0 warning(s)
```

This is an example of a syntax problem that is difficult for linear thought processes (like computers and translators using word-for-word dictionaries) to understand. Slang is another example where syntax may be observed, but direct translation is difficult. If a four-year-old boy came home from pre-school and pronounced, "I am a cool cat." As you might guess, while the syntax is legitimate, the meaning is obscure.

Most beginning programmers run into some linker errors as they develop code, but fortunately, most of these errors are simple because the code being developed is also simple. As you improve your programming skills, you will find that you can generate some complicated linker errors.

To run the build process, you can use the **Build** menu, if you like, first to compile and then build the program (items 1 and 2 on the menu) as seen in Figure 3.38.

Figure 3.38

The Build Menu

```
Build  Tools  Window  Help

  Compile pV.cpp        Ctrl+F7

  Build pV.exe          F7

  Rebuild All

  Batch Build...

  Clean
```

Figure 3.39

The Build Button

This can also be accomplished using the buttons to do a complete build (compile and then build). Once you have worked through the syntax errors, you can move on to the **Build** button shown in Figure 3.39. This has the exact same effect as first choosing **Compile** and then **Build** from the **Build** menu.

Of course, **Rebuild All** is also an option on the **Build** menu (Figure 3.38).

When the linking process begins and linker errors occur, the linker will generate messages starting with LNK to inform you that the error is a linking error and involves some action the compiler didn't expect. From Figure 3.37 we see:

```
PV.obj : error LNK2001: unresolved external symbol "void __cdecl dispSoFar(char * const,int)" (?dispSoFar@@YAXQADH@Z)
Debug/PV.exe : fatal error LNK1120: 1 unresolved externals
```

In the case of Figure 3.37, two errors are actually generated, but they usually are found together. This error is commonly called the link 2001 error and refers to what is called an unresolved external. The message is scary to most beginning programmers, because it contains numerous symbols and cryptic references. There are two keys common to most linker errors: (1) the error message itself and its number, and (2) the name or piece of source code where the error occurred.

If you look carefully, you see **dispSoFar,** a name from the program (refer to Figure 3.37), in this error message. This is a clue that can lead you to the solution of this linker error. The following set of steps can help you work through linker errors. Your instructor may wish to provide additional input on common linker errors encountered in his/her course.

Example 3.3

....

StepsLinker Error

1. Look for clues in the error message with particular regard to lines of source code.

2. Visually examine any line of source code that contains the instruction by using the **Edit, Find** command on the menu. (Copy and paste the information or drag over the phrase, and it will automatically appear in the **Find** box.) These steps are shown in Figures 3.40, 3.41, and 3.42 on the facing page (79).

3. Click **Find Next** and review each line of the program that contains the phrase. In particular, look for misspelling and case errors.

The real focus for basic errors of this type will be on misspelling and case violations. This is usually the case with LNK 2001 errors because they refer to a name that is legal, but has no instructions associated with it. There are many other linker errors you may encounter, but this method may help you at least zero in on the lines where these errors are occurring.

Figure 3.40

The Copy and
Paste

Figure 3.41

The Edit, Find
Command

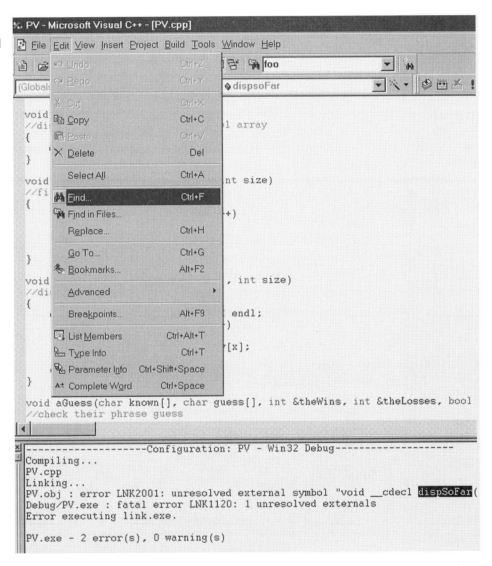

Figure 3.42

The Find Box

The bad news is there may be large numbers of lines that fall into this category. Hopefully, in your beginning programming class, most of the linker errors you encounter will fall into the LNK 2001 type and be resolvable using the error steps above. If you are encountering unusual errors, be sure and point them out to your instructor so he or she can be aware of the problem. It is likely happening to others in the class as well.

Disk Space Errors

One last problem worthy of mention is the scarcity of space. In the real world, programmers usually develop on systems where they have rights and privileges and can use the hard drive or other large storage media for work. Students often have no rights and privileges in labs and may be forced to use less desirable means of storage, such as a floppy disk. If the compiler runs out of space during any portion of the compile or linking process, an error will occur. The errors do not say, Out of disk space but may say something like Fatal Error, cannot access. Figure 3.43 and Figure 3.44 demonstrate a clue and an error resulting from a full floppy disk.

The clue is the compiler telling you that some files are not going to be available for viewing. This won't prevent the program from compiling, but it is usually a tip-off that you are running out of disk space.

Figure 3.44 contains a fatal error that is the direct result of a full disk. The compiler can only tell that there is something wrong with one of the files used in the process. It has no idea what this problem is. Unfortunately, this error can be a wide variety of things based upon, whether the source code was compiled previously (if, for example, you had it working and then saved your term paper on the same disk); where in the process the disk filled up; or whether or not certain files were created. Thus, Figure 3.44 is not an accurate guide to error messages of this type, but merely an example of this problem as it occurs. Essentially, if you receive strange fatal errors during the compile/linking process that involve missing, obsolete, or corrupted files, this usually means the disk is full.

Figure 3.43

The Clue to a Full Floppy Disk

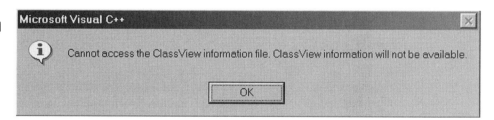

Figure 3.44

A Full Disk Fatal Error

```
--------------------Configuration: myFirstCpp - Win32 Debug--------------------
Compiling...
Command line warning D4028 : minimal rebuild failure, reverting to normal build
myFirstCpp.cpp
a:\myfirstcpp.cpp(0) : fatal error C1051: program database file, 'a:\debug\vc60.pdb', has an obsolete format, delete it and recompile
Error executing cl.exe.

myFirstCpp.exe - 1 error(s), 1 warning(s)
```

As suggested earlier in this book, if you are forced to use floppy disks for your programs, use a separate disk for each one. This should provide plenty of space for most programming assignments at this level. Also, don't forget to make backup copies. Floppy disks are notorious for failing and/or being eaten by your pet snake just before the assignment is due.

Executing the Program

Finally, you have reached the point where you can smugly click **Rebuild All** on the **Build** menu and watch as no errors occur. This is usually accompanied by lots of celebratory dancing and shouts of "thank you thank you thank you." When you have successfully "rebuilt all" and created the **.exe** file with your program, you can finally proceed to execute the program using either the **Execute** button or the **Build** menu.

The **Execute** button is an exclamation mark, as shown in Figure 3.45.

The **Build** menu has an **Execute** item you can click as seen in Figure 3.46.

The **Execute** menu item will have the name of the current file specified on it, so it won't look exactly like Figure 3.46.

Figure 3.45

The Execute Button

Figure 3.46

Execution from the Build Menu

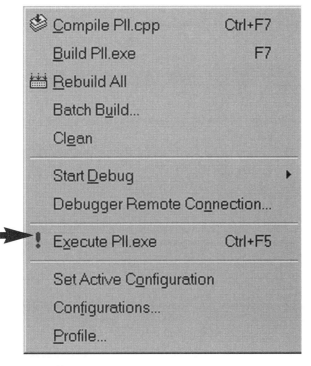

You might also press **CTRL-F5** (hold down the **Control** key and press the **F5** function key simultaneously). This is also noted on the Execute menu item shown in Figure 3.46.

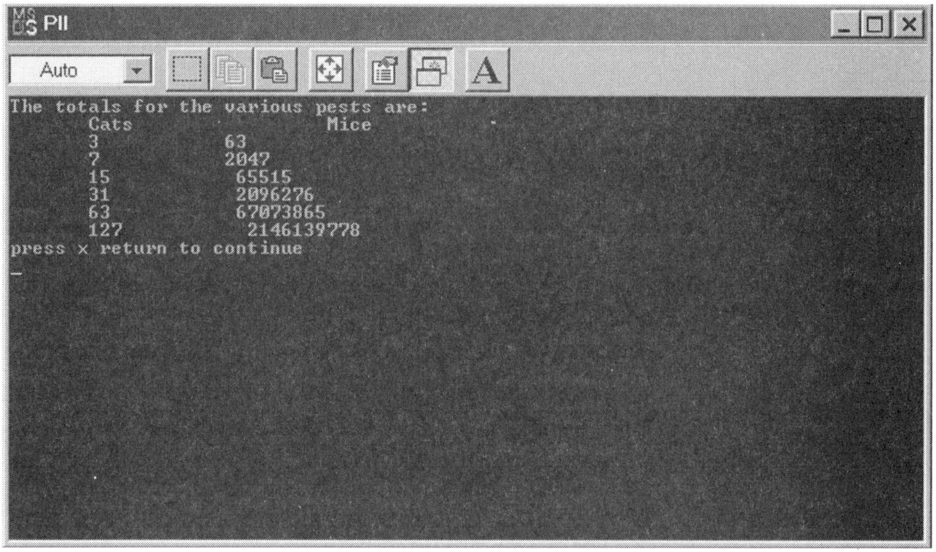

Figure 3.47

The DOS Execution Window

At this point, the program will run correctly, will run but contain covert logic errors, or will run and contain overt logic errors. Many C++ programs will run in a DOS window as shown in Figure 3.47.

The DOS window will contain instructions to the user, requests for data and results, of the operations being conducted by the C++ instructions in the source code.

Logic Errors

Many beginning programmers feel that when they finally get an **.exe** file built, their job is done and they can go and collect their A on the assignment. Unfortunately, errors can occur here as well. These are called logic errors and are categorized two ways: (1) overt logic errors and (2) covert logic errors.

Overt logic errors are problems in your program that result in something that is obviously a problem happening. This is not the same as a syntax or linker error in that the program is actually running, but something is still obviously wrong.

Let's use an example of a symphony orchestra. Suppose everyone is playing a Bach concerto except for the trombone player, who accidentally got a copy of Dixieland Rag. This can be compared to a syntax error like we saw earlier. Now, suppose everyone gets the music straightened out. The trombone player now has a copy of the Bach concerto, but his trombone is badly out of tune. He's playing the right notes, but it's painfully obvious that something is wrong. This might be analogous to an overt logic error.

Closer to home, imagine you walk up to an ATM machine and put in all the information to withdraw $20. Suppose the programmer accidentally forgot to have the machine log you out and return your card! This would not cause a syntax or linker error. It is a valid instruction (or lack of an instruction), but it would certainly be an obvious problem.

Covert logic errors are problems in your program that result in less-than-obvious errors. Suppose that in our symphony example, the trombone player is now playing the Bach concerto but has received the wrong music and is playing the part written for a bass. The music is correct and it may difficult for someone who is not an expert to figure out what is wrong. In the case of the ATM, imagine if instead of $20 falling into the hopper, $200 falls out, but only $20 is deducted from your account. This problem will be difficult to detect even with an accounting audit because there is no record of where the money went.

Spotting an Overt Logic Error

Now that your program is running, you should be able to spot strange occurrences just by working with it. As you practice programming by doing it, you will learn to spot problems and anomalous behavior, but even experienced programmers sometimes miss problems. Learn to look for strange things. Try different approaches to running your code that will force these errors to reveal themselves to you instead of to an end-user who has purchased your program. In Chapter 4, the Step debugger is introduced to help you work through both overt and covert logic errors in your code.

Chapter 3 Exercises

1. Return to the **myFirstCpp** program you created in Chapter 2 and compile and execute it. If you are lucky there will be no errors, but you probably will encounter some. See if you can remove them all using the methods described in this chapter.

2. Open the file **debug2.cpp** from the accompanying CD and work on this file. There are many syntax errors in this program for you to work on and remove. If you can remove them, all, you will have started to develop some real syntax debugging skills.

3. Try and create some errors on your own. Use the debug1 program you used for the tutorial in this chapter. See if you can create all the errors discussed in the chapter intentionally. This will give you some experience with the different types of errors and what they look like in a program.

4 Using the Step Debugger

All programmers experience errors, all of them. All programmers must deal with logic errors, all of them. Overt and covert logic errors are the bane of all programmers' lives, because they are difficult to detect and even more difficult to resolve. Logic errors may be the result of an incorrect value (like say pi = 3 instead of 3.14...) or a source code that calls the wrong process at the wrong time (like turning on the heat instead of the air conditioning). The larger the project, the more difficult it will be to narrow down where these problems originate.

One of the best tools for uncovering logic errors and for testing to make sure the problems are non-existent, is the Step Debugger. This tool allows programmers to execute their code one line at a time and even allows for looking at the values of variables, and so forth, during the pause. This powerful tool will enable you to locate problems and correct them.

Unfortunately, the Step Debugger cannot help you with syntax problems. It also requires that an executable file be created before the debugger will run. Thus, you will have to resort to the measures discussed in chapters 2 and 3 to resolve all the other problems before you can deal with any logic errors that may be plaguing you.

Step Execution.

For this chapter we will first be working with a file called stepdebug1.cpp. Create a new subdirectory called step on your hard drive. You can copy it from the book disk into this subdirectory.*

The stepdebug1.cpp source code contains some errors that will be good examples in the Step Debugger process. You may wish to wait for your instructor to assign this chapter because it involves more advanced programming concepts that you may not understand on Day 1 (or even Day 10). You might also refer to your C++ textbook for references to this material.

---

* If you are unsure how to do this, refer back to the earlier tutorials that walk you through the creation of subdirectories.

Step Debugger Tutorial, Part I

····················

1. Copy the program stepdebug1.cpp onto your disk and then open it.

2. You should then see the program appear in the editing window just as in the previous tutorials.

3. First, compile the program by clicking the **Rebuild all** button. You can answer **Yes** to use the default workspace.

4. The program should compile without any errors or warnings. (See Figure 4.1.)

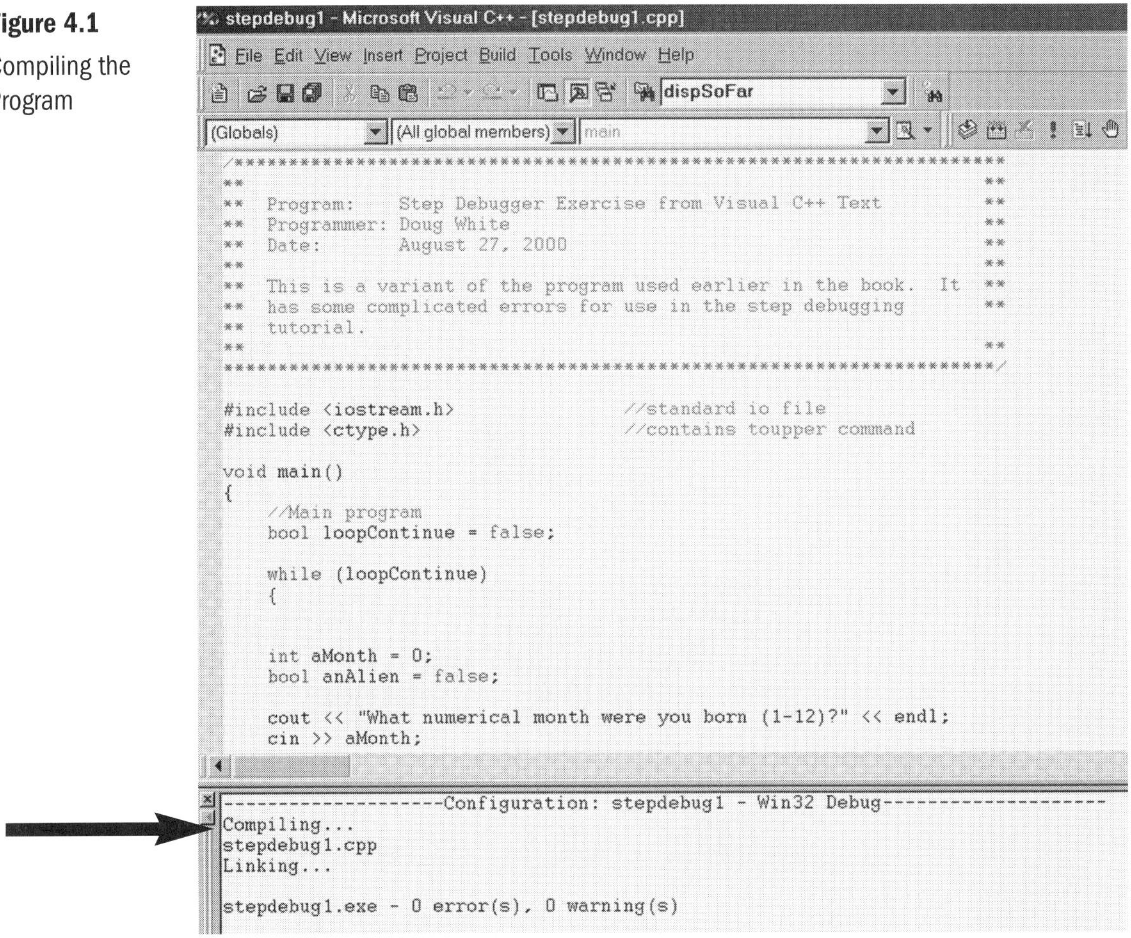

Figure 4.1

Compiling the Program

Figure 4.2

Program Runs

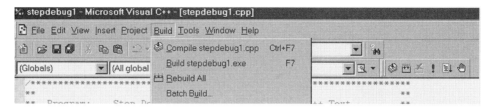

Figure 4.3

Running the
Debugger

```
/*******************************************************************
**                                                               **
**   Program:      Step Debugger Exercise from Visual C++ Text    **
**   Programmer: Doug White                                       **
**   Date:          August 27, 2000                               **
**                                                               **
**   This is a variant of the program used earlier in the book.  It  **
**   has some complicated errors for use in the step debugging    **
**   tutorial.                                                    **
**                                                               **
*******************************************************************/

#include <iostream.h>              //standard io file
#include <ctype.h>                 //contains toupper command

void main()
{
    //Main program
    bool loopContinue = false;

    while (loopContinue)
    {

        int aMonth = 0;
        bool anAlien = false;

        cout << "What numerical month were you born (1-12)?" << endl;
        cin >> aMonth;

        switch (aMonth)               //test the data
        {
        case 1:
```

5. Run the program . Surprisingly, you should see that nothing happens(Figure 4.2).

6. Press the space bar or **Return** to continue. You should return to the Visual C++ editing window.

7. The program must have at least one logic error. It doesn't do what you expected. Thus, the best approach is to use the step debugger to see what is happening in the program.

8. Click on the **Build** menu, **Start Debug**, and **Step Into** your program. (See Figure 4.3.)

Figure 4.4

The Next Line Indicator

```
/*********************************************************************
**                                                                 **
**   Program:     Step Debugger Exercise from Visual C++ Text       **
**   Programmer: Doug White                                         **
**   Date:         August 27, 2000                                  **
**                                                                 **
**   This is a variant of the program used earlier in the book.  It **
**   has some complicated errors for use in the step debugging      **
**   tutorial.                                                      **
**                                                                 **
*********************************************************************/

#include <iostream.h>              //standard io file
#include <ctype.h>                 //contains toupper command

void main()
{
    //Main program
    bool loopContinue = false;

    while (loopContinue)
    {

        int aMonth = 0;
        bool anAlien = false;

        cout << "What numerical month were you born (1-12)?" << endl;
        cin >> aMonth;

        switch (aMonth)            //test the data
        {
        case 1:
```

9. This will actually start the program running but will only execute the first line. You need to use **Step Into** at this point because you have no breakpoints in the code. You will see a small yellow arrow (Figure 4.4), which indicates the next line of code that will be executed. The debugger will take care of any preprocessing (includes) and skip into the main program.

The Stepping Options

The Build menu has now changed to the **Debug** menu. If you will open that menu, you will see several options for executing the program. (See Figure 4.5.) The five main options that you will use are **Go, Step Into, Step Over, Step Out,** and **Run to Cursor**.

Go (F5)

The **Go** option tells the debugger to run. This means that if you have no breakpoints in the code, the program will run to its completion. Use this option when you have set some breakpoints in the program and you want to get to them (or between them) quickly.

Step Into (F11)

This is a more complex option that allows the programmer to enter a function or other command instead of just processing it. If you are working through a program that has function calls, or if you want to see what is happening inside the function, you must use **Step Into** or the function will simply execute and you will be on the line following the function call in the main program. Basically, any call that places the cursor outside of "main" will require **Step Into** if you want to see the underlying function. This is handy if you want to skip a function you know works, particularly functions included with the compiler. If the line is not a function call, **Step Into** executes the current line and moves to the next. Don't use this command except to enter your own functions because it is very easy to end up in the C++ sub-strata, which will be confusing. If you do end up in the C++ functions, just hit Shift-F11, which will return you to main.

Step Over (F10)

You use this item most in the debugger as it just steps "over" the current line. This doesn't keep the line from executing, just steps over it. It also executes functions calls and so forth without showing you all the underlying steps that are used to run the function.

Step Out (Shift-F11)

Step Out is the opposite of **Step Into**. If you find yourself in a function or C++ sub-strata and don't want to be there, just press shift-f11 and you will return up to the portion of the code that called that function. The remainder of the function will execute, you just won't see it all happen. This is useful if you think a certain function may be causing problems and after a few steps realize it is not the source.

Run to Cursor (Ctrl-F10)

This command simply executes the program up to wherever the user has placed the cursor in the program. This is useful if you do not wish to set a breakpoint in the program. Some people prefer to use this option instead of setting breakpoints.

Figure 4.5

The Debugger Stepping Options

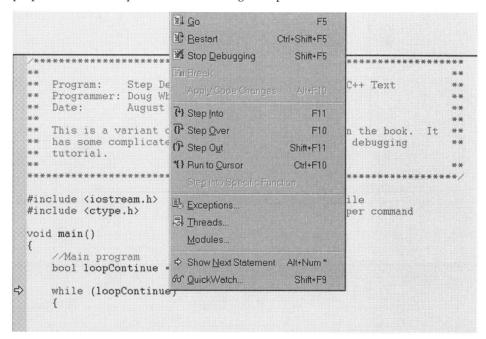

Inserting and Removing Breakpoints

Before you use the step debugger, you may want to review the source code, try to identify the general area in which the errors are occurring. This is done by using the Insert **Breakpoint** button or the **Debugger** menu. Breakpoints allow you to get to interesting pieces of the code quickly without stepping, a line at a time, through hundreds of lines of source code that are not of interest. The tutorial will show you how to insert and remove some breakpoints in the stepdebug1 program. Remember that breakpoints have no impact on your program other than how it executes, so don't worry about using them or deleting them at will.

Breakpoints are inserted by right-clicking the mouse on the line where you want to insert or remove the breakpoint. A right-click will open the Debugger menu (see Figure 4.6) and allow you to manipulate breakpoints on this line of the source code.

You can more easily insert breakpoints by clicking the Breakpoint button on the main menu bar. This button is seen in Figure 4.7. Clicking the button when the current line is a non-breakpoint line inserts a breakpoint; clicking it when the current line already has a breakpoint will remove the breakpoint.

You can tell when a breakpoint exists because you will see a large red dot next to the line of source code, as shown in Figure 4.8.

Figure 4.6

The Breakpoint Menu

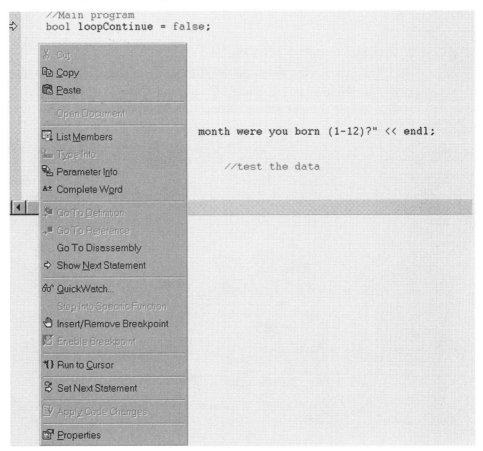

Figure 4.7

The Breakpoint
Button

```
stepdebug1 - Microsoft Visual C++ [break] - [stepdebug1.cpp *]
File Edit View Insert Project Debug Tools Window Help
```
dispSoFar

(Globals)   (All global members)   main

Figure 4.8

The Breakpoint
Indicator

```
#include <iostream.h>                //standard io file
#include <ctype.h>                   //contains toupper command

void main()
{
    //Main program
    bool loopContinue = true;

    while (loopContinue)
    {

        int aMonth = 0;
        bool anAlien = false;

        cout << "What numerical month were you born (1-12)?" << endl;
        cin >> aMonth;

        switch (aMonth)              //test the data
        {
        case 1:
            {
                cout << "Garnet ";
                break;
```

Step Debugger Tutorial, Part II

1. Your cursor (the yellow arrow) should be pointing to the first line of the main program, which starts `bool`.
2. Press the **F10** key and the cursor will step over to the next line, `while`.
3. The line `bool` has been executed.
4. The current line, `while,` is now waiting to be executed. Press **F10** again.
5. The cursor jumps to the last line of the entire program. This is a major clue to the first logic error in the program.
6. Since the line `while`, seems to be the last line executed, let's set a breakpoint there.
7. Click on the line `while` and press the **Breakpoint** button. (See Figure 4.9.)

Figure 4.9

Inserting a
Breakpoint

```
#include <iostream.h>                //standard io file
#include <ctype.h>                   //contains toupper command

void main()
{
    //Main program
    bool loopContinue = false;

    while (loopContinue)
    {
```

8. This will cause the debugger to stop here when the program runs. You will need to restart the program first however. Open the debugger menu and choose **Restart**, as shown in Figure 4.10.

9. The yellow cursor will now return to the first line of the main program. You can press **F5** (Go) to jump down to the breakpoint. Press **F5**.

10. This is a loop call for a while loop that is controlled by the value of the Boolean, `loopContinue`. If the Boolean is true, then the loop runs or continues to run. If the Boolean is false, the loop stops. Check the value of the Boolean by setting up a watch on this variable. This is done using the **Watch** window pane in the lower right corner. You can add the variable `loopContinue` to the **Watch** pane by simply typing its name in on the first line, as shown in Figure 4.11.

Figure 4.10

Restarting the Program

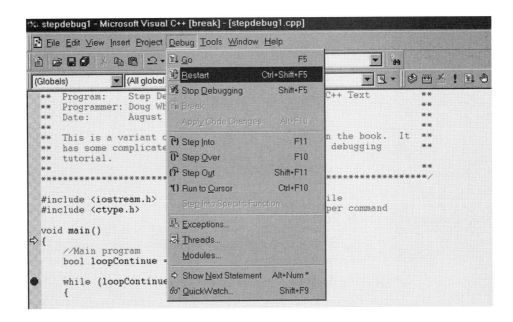

Figure 4.11

The Watch Pane

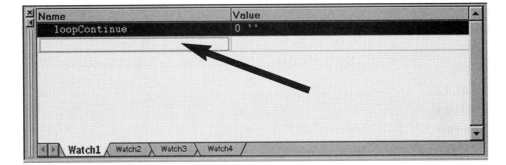

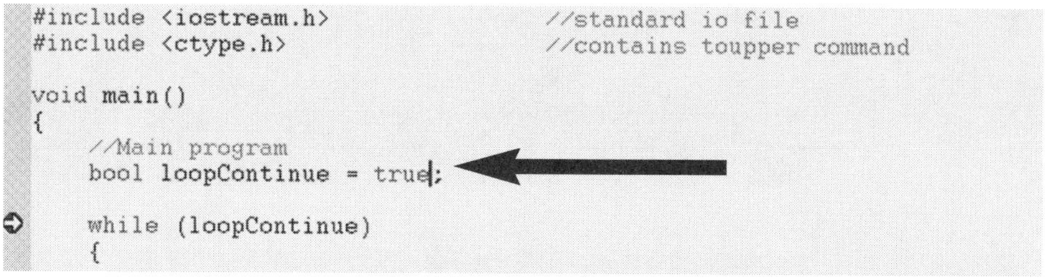

Figure 4.12

Changing a Value

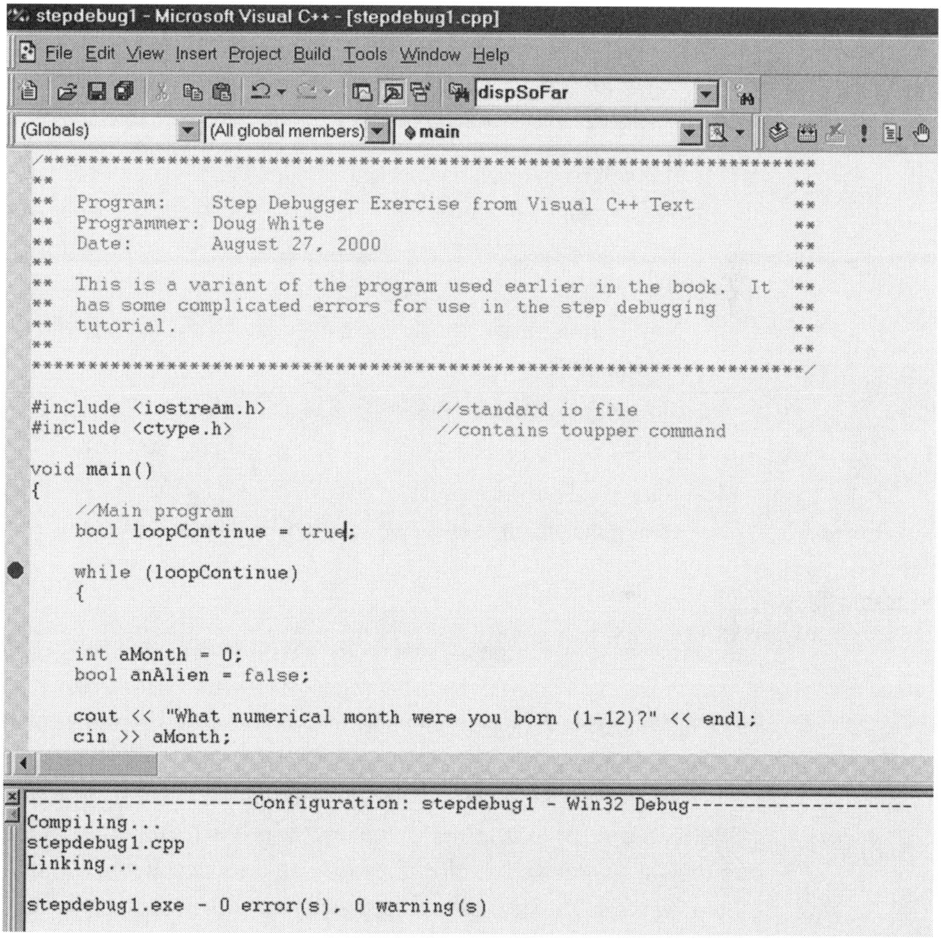

```
#include <iostream.h>                //standard io file
#include <ctype.h>                   //contains toupper command

void main()
{
    //Main program
    bool loopContinue = true;    ⬅====
    
    while (loopContinue)
    {
```

Figure 4.13

The Save,
Recompile, and
Successful
Recompile

```
stepdebug1 - Microsoft Visual C++ - [stepdebug1.cpp]
File  Edit  View  Insert  Project  Build  Tools  Window  Help

(Globals)          (All global members)   ◆ main

/***************************************************************
**                                                           **
**   Program:     Step Debugger Exercise from Visual C++ Text  **
**   Programmer: Doug White                                   **
**   Date:        August 27, 2000                             **
**                                                           **
**   This is a variant of the program used earlier in the book. It **
**   has some complicated errors for use in the step debugging  **
**   tutorial.                                                **
**                                                           **
***************************************************************/

#include <iostream.h>                //standard io file
#include <ctype.h>                   //contains toupper command

void main()
{
    //Main program
    bool loopContinue = true;

    while (loopContinue)
    {


    int aMonth = 0;
    bool anAlien = false;

    cout << "What numerical month were you born (1-12)?" << endl;
    cin >> aMonth;

--------------------Configuration: stepdebug1 - Win32 Debug--------------------
Compiling...
stepdebug1.cpp
Linking...

stepdebug1.exe - 0 error(s), 0 warning(s)
```

11. This will now "watch" the variable's value while the program runs. Note that its current value is 0, false. This tells the programmer the loop will never run.

12. The programmer must then decide why the value is false. Look at the variable's initialization; it is set to false—an obvious error that resulted in a bizarre outcome. Change the value of the initialization of loopContinue to true, as shown in Figure 4.12.

Figure 4.14

Enter 9

Figure 4.15

The Successful
Run

13. This will require you to resave the program and recompile. All this can be accomplished using the button bars (see Figure 4.13 on the previous page) as you have learned earlier. When you save, you will be warned that the debugger will stop. Click **OK**.

14. Now, you should run the program again and see what happens. Click the **Execute** or **Go** button (!)

15. The program will ask you for the month in which you were born (see Figure 4.14). Just for example, use September. Type **9**, and press **Return**.

16. You should see the message, "Sapphire is your birthstone!" and be offered the option to continue, as shown in Figure 4.15. Choose **y** and press **Return**.

Program Testing

Commercial programs are tested thousands of times by different people to determine if any errors exist. Imagine your embarrassment when your program requires the release of a patch. Despite programmers' desires to release error-free code, problems that were never tested may slip through.

Using test data is one approach to determining where errors exist. In the tutorial so far, we have done what is called "sampling," which is testing some of the functionality of the program but not all. It is often the case with commercial products that not all the potential problems can be tested, given the deadlines and desires of the company. Thus, sampling may be used with the assumption that if 50 percent (or some established percentage) of the functions work, all the rest will probably work.

If possible however, companies prefer exhaustive, or "population," testing. This means that every possible option is tested before the program is released. This may take a great deal of time, but it will reduce the number of patches needed later.

Step Debugger Tutorial, Part III
··················

Our program so far seems to work with our 8 percent sample (1/12). Let's test the program exhaustively.

1. If your program is still running from Part II just continue, otherwise execute your program again.

2. Work through the entire numerical sequence (1–12) for all the birthstones and see if you find any anomalies.

3. 10 doesn't work. (See Figure 4.16.) It looks like people born in October are out of luck with this program.

4. There must be an error somewhere in the source code causing such a problem. Again, the step debugger can help. Choose **n** to stop your program and start the debugger with **Step Into**.

5. Since everything seems to work until the program decides on the month, let's set a breakpoint at the beginning of the switch statement where the decisions are made. You may want to remove the breakpoint on the `while` line since the while loop seems **OK** at this point. (See Figure 4.17.)

Figure 4.16

The Problem with October

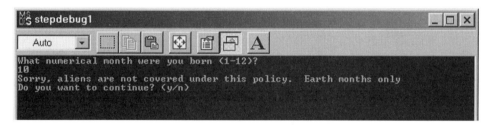

Figure 4.17

Inserting and Removing Breakpoints again

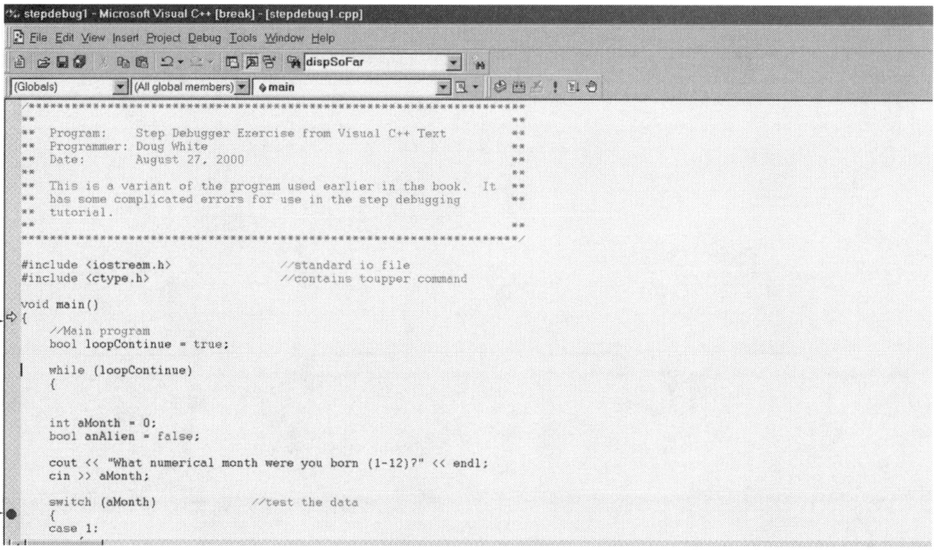

Figure 4.18

The Go (or Execute)
Button

Figure 4.19

Program Questions
in the DOS Window

Figure 4.20

Selecting a
Variable with the
Mouse

```
    switch (aMonth)                 //test the data
    {
    case 1:
        {
            cout << "Garnet ";
            break;
```

Figure 4.21

QuickWatch

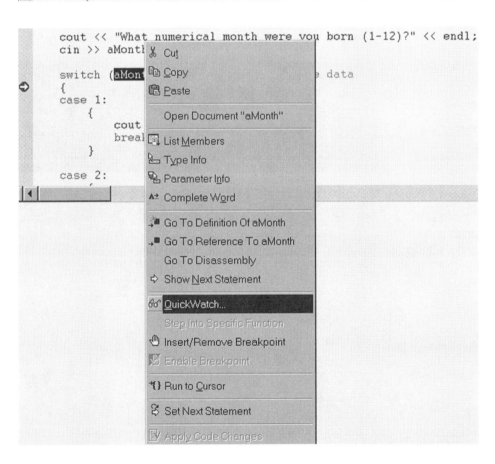

6. Now you can run the program down to the breakpoint. Click the **Go** button (see Figure 4.18) or press F5 to run down to the breakpoint.

7. Answer the questions that appear in the program's DOS window. We are interested in October, so enter **10** and press **Return** when the window appears (see Figure 4.19).

8. The program will stop at the breakpoint you set and now you can step through. Let's verify the variable by using a **QuickWatch** (or you can add it to the **Watch** pane as in Part II).

9. Hold down the left mouse button and drag over the variable. This will select the variable `aMonth`, as shown in Figure 4.20.

10. Now, right-click the mouse and a menu appears. Choose **QuickWatch** on the menu, as in Figure 4.21.

11. The **QuickWatch** pane will appear. See Figure 4.22.

Figure 4.22

The QuickWatch Pane

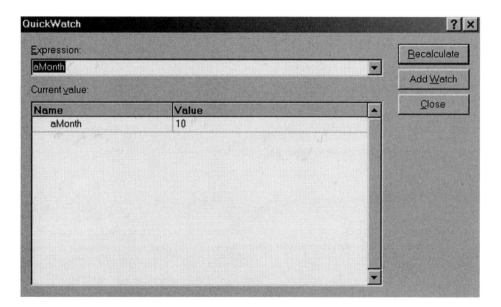

12. If you will look at the value of the variable as shown in Figure 4.23 on the following page, you see it is "10," which is what you presumed it to be. This means the error is somewhere else, but at least we know the variable was input correctly.

13. Although the variable is correct on this line, something could change it; so let's add it to the **Watch** pane so that we can track it as the program runs. Click the **Add Watch** button (see Figure 4.23) on the **QuickWatch** pane.

Figure 4.23

The Variable Value

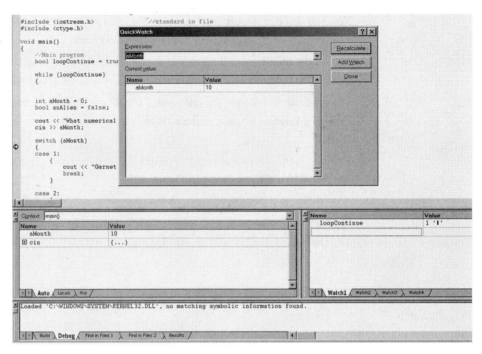

Figure 4.24

The Add Watch

14. `aMonth` will appear in the **Watch** pane in the lower right-hand corner of the screen, as shown in Figure 4.25.

15. Now, let's step a line at a time using **Step Over** (F10) and see what happens. Press **F10**.

Figure 4.25

The Watch pane

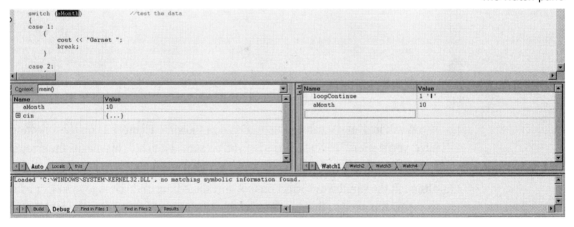

16. The program jumps to the default section of the choices, as shown in Figure 4.26.

17. That would imply that the case 10 section was skipped. Move up and look at the line for the 10 option above, as shown in Figure 4.27.

Figure 4.26

The Default Section of the Program

```
default:
    {
        //something is wrong
        cout << "Sorry, aliens are not covered
        //main();                    //start over
        anAlien = true;
        break;
```

Figure 4.27

The 10 section

```
case 9:
    {
            cout << "Sapphire ";
            break;
    }
case 19:
    {
            cout << "Opal ";
            break;
    }
case 11:
    {
            cout << "Topaz ";
            break;
    }
```

Figure 4.28

Replace the 9 with a 0

```
case 10:
    {
            cout << "Opal ";
```

18. Hmmm, it's set to 19, as Figure 4.27 shows. Perhaps the programmer accidentally typed **9** instead of **0** (they are close together on the keyboard).

19. Correct the error by deleting the **9** and replacing it with a **0** (see Figure 4.28).

20. **Save** and **Recompile** using the button bar.

21. You should again get the error-free compile.

This completes the tutorial on the **Step Debugger**. This powerful tool will help you in both testing and debugging logic errors.

Chapter 4 Exercises

1. Use the Step Debugger to work through the logic problems in **stepdebug2.cpp**, which is on your disk.

   ....

2. Use the Step Debugger to work through the logic problems in **stepdebug3.cpp**, which is on your disk.

   ....

5 The Creation of Workspaces

U p to this point in the book, we have been working with individual Visual C++ source codes. You may recall that when we compiled the tutorial, Visual C++ asked about a default workspace for the source code. Visual C++ compiles all source codes in a workspace, even if the source code consists of a single file. This is because a Visual C++ program is made up of a number of different files (as we saw during the compilation process), debug space, and other files used by the compiler. Visual C++ bundles all the files used for a program together into an area called a workspace.

This chapter focuses on setting up workspaces for your programs in your programming course. The workspace provides a more efficient means of managing multi-part programs and/or programs that need additional instructions (called **header** or **.h** files) in order to function.

Workspace versus Project Space

Definition 5.1

A workspace is an area where all source codes and other files used in a program are stored together with their object files and executables.

For your information, Visual C++ also incorporates the idea of a project space. Project spaces are more elaborate workspaces designed for specialized programming tasks, such as the development of simple Windows programs (like a backgammon game), interfacing with a database (an airline ticketing application), or designing a huge stand-alone application for an operating system (Microsoft Word).

Definition 5.2

A project space is an area where all the specialized tools, including drivers, files, programs, and other tools are brought together to design a specific application.

So, what's the difference between a project space and a workspace? A project space is dedicated to a specific task, whereas a workspace is simply an area that can be used generically. An analogy might be to a surgical suite at hospital. The workspace would be an operating room that is ready but has not been prepared for any particular procedure. A surgical team could arrive and assemble the equipment necessary for a specialized task, but it would take some time. The project space is a room that has been prepared for a specific operation. All the tools and equipment have been assembled and are waiting for an expert to come and put them to use. This type of project development is beyond the scope of this text, but you should keep in mind that these tools exist.

Header Files

One of the many advantages of object-oriented programming (a theoretical and practical approach to programming used by C++) is the use of files written by other programmers and shared with everyone. A simple example in C++ programming is the need for exponents in mathematics. The standard C++ compiler does not contain any instruction that will allow a programmer to write an exponential term like x^2, thus, every programmer would have to develop code to allow the use of exponents in a program. While developing a way to handle exponents is an interesting assignment, it is not easy task. Over time, many programs have been coded and are now included with C++ compilers. The files that contain these instructions are called header files or .h files. They are specialized C++ programs that can be "included" with your program in one of two forms.

Companies often develop header files to solve common programming tasks. A bank, for example, may have header files for computing interest or the price of a bond for an investor. Programmers at the bank can save themselves time by simply reusing these files.

Header files may be stored on a disk and loaded when the program is compiled. This type of inclusion means that if the source code is to be shared with others, the entire header files (and any other files) will need to be bundled together somehow and shared as well. This type of operation often leads to lost and missing files and subsequent problems for users of your source code.

Header files may also be included with your source code as a part of the workspace. In this case, the workspace will contain all the files needed to compile your source code and can readily be exchanged. The advantage is simply organization.

Which is better? Well, if your program is only being distributed as an executable file, then everything is already there. The advantage to using workspace header files is seen when many programmers are sharing a programming project. (Don't confuse this with a project space.) Including the header files insures that all of the collaborators will have access to the multi-component source code.

Creation of Workspaces Tutorial

It is to the programmer's advantage to use workspaces to store all the files for a given project. This allows a programmer to open all the files at the same time (by opening the workspace), compile all the files together, and generally, maintain the files in an organized fashion. It also allows him or her to close all the files that are open for that workspace at the same time in order to work on a different or new problem.

In this tutorial, we will create a workspace, add some files to the workspace, and then compile them.

1. Start Visual C++.

2. Choose the **File New** menu. (See Figure 5.1.)

Figure 5.1   The File New Menu

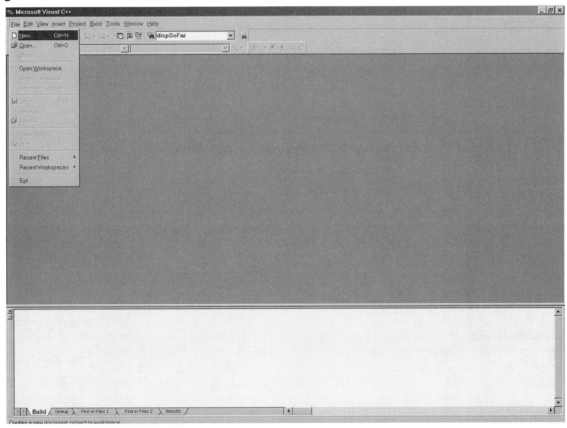

3. This will open the **New** box, which will allow you to pick what you want to create. The default is the **Projects** tab. Click on **Workspaces** to see the options (Figure 5.2).
4. The workspace options are simple and only include blank workspaces at this point. In the name area, type **workspace1** as the name of this project and then, in the directory area, enter the **cppFun** directory you created earlier, as in Figure 5.3. You may store the files anywhere you like but the tutorial will assume the **cppFun** directory.

Figure 5.2

The Workspace Options

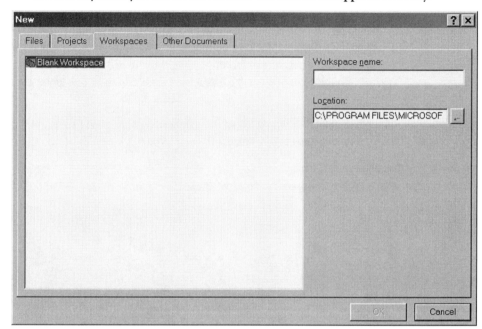

Figure 5.3

The Workspace Name

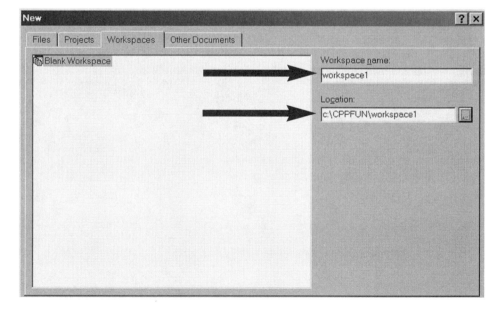

6.   Click **OK** and the workspace will be created for you. This looks like the area you worked in previously, but now all the files contained here are a part of the workspace **workspace1**. This will allow you to manage files efficiently.

7.   At this point, notice the changes to the **File** menu (Figure 5.4). The menu now contains three options to manage your workspace, **Open**, **Save**, and **Close**.

8.   Open will open another workspace, Save will save the current workspace and all the files in that workspace, and **Close** will close the current workspace.

9.   At this point, anything you create—a source code, a header file, or a project space— can be included into the workspace. When you are done with the workspace, close it. You will be asked to verify that all files are to be closed.

Figure 5.4

The Workspace/
File Menu

Figure 5.5
The Close all Documents Box

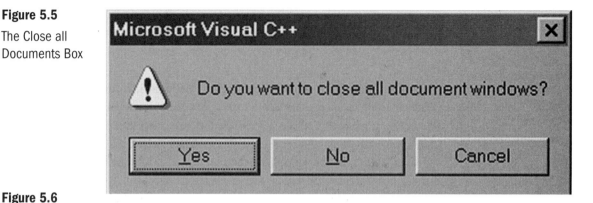

Figure 5.6
The Workspace1 Subdirectory

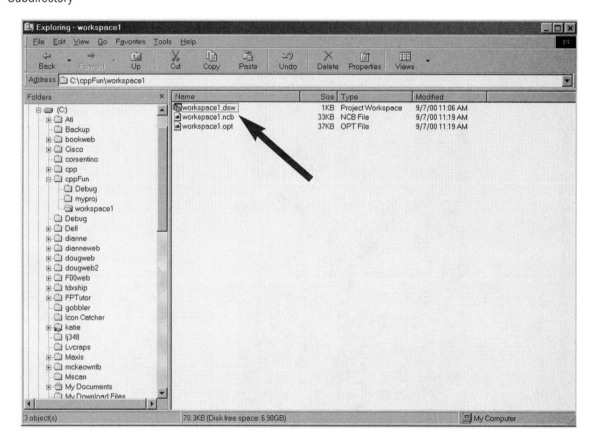

10. Clicking **Yes** will close everything in the workspace. (See Figure 5.5.)
11. You may notice that all the workspace files are now managed in a subdirectory, which was automatically created, called **workspace1** (see Figure 5.6). It contains a file with the **.dsw** extension that actually houses all the workspace items.

Using the Workspace

Once you have created a workspace, using it is much the same as using an isolated source code in Visual C++. You can compile, edit, or delete the files that are contained in the workspace. The real advantage is that all the files are now bundled together. As you proceed in your C++ course, you will see that the inclusion of header files and multi-source-code files is greatly facilitated when they are all contained in one easy to manage area.

6 Options in Visual C++

The final chapter of this book covers setting some of the options in the Visual C++ package you are using. Students regularly use the package with the default settings, but you may wish to modify the defaults to meet your own needs or the wishes of your instructor.

The Options Menu

All of the options that can be set for the environment are found on the **Options** menu. You can open this window by choosing the **Tools Options** menu (Figure 6.1).

Figure 6.1

The Tools Options Menu

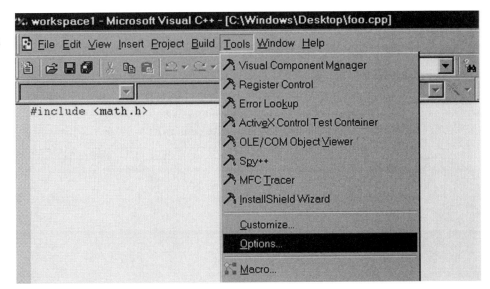

Once you select **Options** the **Options** box will appear. See Figure 6.2.

This box allows you to choose all the different settings available in the Visual C++ package.

Figure 6.2

The Options Box, Tabs Tab

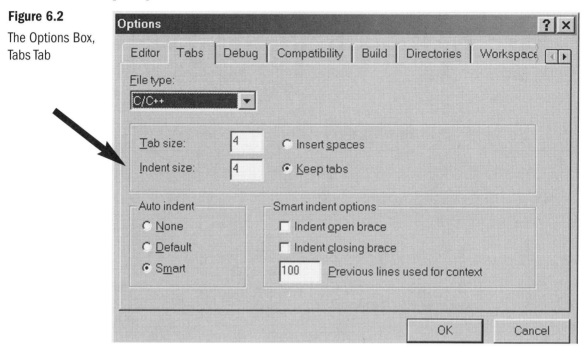

Setting Indentations and Tabs

Click on the **Tabs** tab and you will see the controls for the size of both tabs and indentations in the environment. The arrow points to these controls in Figure 6.2. The default setting, for C/C++, uses conventional tabbing and indents for this type of program.

This section also contains "smart" indents, which can be set to indent curly braces ({}).

The other important feature here is the ability to set tabs by spaces as opposed to "tabs." In most PC environments, word processing programs allow for tabs and can manage them. In ASCII text files, which are commonly encountered in UNIX or LINUX environments, tabs may not be supported and spaces will need to be used. This is likely the most important option you need to be aware of in Visual C++ at this point in your programming. If you plan to port your source codes onto other platforms as ASCII text files, it is strongly recommended you use spaces instead of tabs. Note that because C++ ignores whitespace—in this case the tabs—spaces should not affect your compile, only the appearance of your source code.

Default Directories

As you develop your programming skills, you may wish to set additional directories to be searched for header files, source codes, and so forth. This is done using the **Directories** tab on the **Options** box. Click the **Directories** tab, as shown in Figure 6.3.

Figure 6.3

The Directories Tab

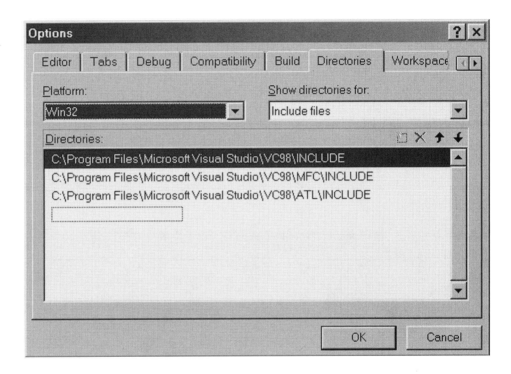

This will allow you to see which directories are currently being searched for header files, source codes, and so forth when the compiler works with your workspaces and source code. If you wish to add directories to this list, click the **New** button to add them. See Figure 6.4 on the following page for an example.

Figure 6.4

New Directories

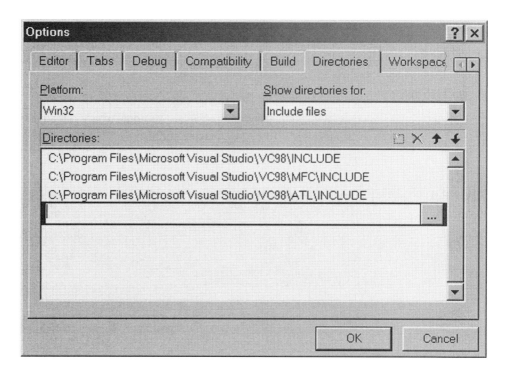

Figure 6.5

The Browse Button
and Directory
Browse Box

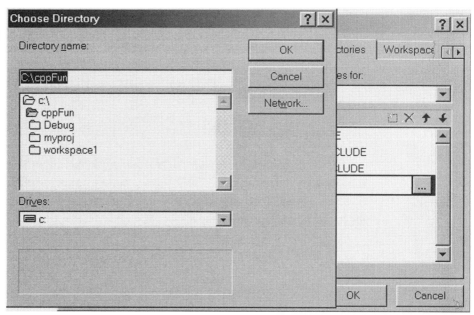

A box will appear to allow you type in the directory or you can click on the ... button to browse the directories that exist on any drives to which you have access. The ... button and resulting browser box are illustrated in Figure 6.5.

There are many other options and features that may be managed in the Visual C++ environment. Overall, the environment represents a powerful tool for both beginning and expert programmers. As you continue to study programming in the C++ language, explore all the options to maximize your experience. Your instructor may wish to provide additional information about specific features he/she wishes to use in your course.

INDEX